D1472397

The Essential Guide to Selling Your Home

How to Sell Your Home for the Most Amount of Money in the Shortest Amount of Time!

Richard J. Cordaro

"The Essential Guide to Selling Your Home: How to Sell Your Home for the Most Amount of Money in the Shortest Amount of Time!" by Richard Cordaro

Interior Graphics | Jessica Woken

Editing & Layout
Mountain Owl Ink, LLC | Minnesota, USA

Cover Art | Courtesy 99Designs.com

Distributed and Printed through Amazon KDP
ISBN 978-1-9805-7809-3

For permissions contact
RCordaroBooks@gmail.com

To my amazing children, Christopher and Laura:

You have been a blessing in my life and continue to inspire me.
From you I've learned more than I could ever teach.
You make me proud.

I love you both so much.

- Dad.

Acknowledgements

I would like to express gratitude to my editor, Jessica Woken, for her patience, creativity, and her way with words. I would also like to congratulate her on the birth of her son who arrived during this book's writing. I have a new appreciation for nap times.

I would like to thank Joy and Chris Daniels, Janice Santoni, and all of the great staff at the Joy Daniels Real Estate Group. You are the best of the best!

A special thanks to James Spooner who motivates me to dream big and to know that I can do anything I set my mind upon.

I am proud to be associated with my students, fellow staff, and colleagues of Harrisburg Area Community College who inspire and motivate me to do and be my best.

Many thanks to my past clients who I have had the pleasure of meeting and working with. You have been wonderful and have made this book possible by giving me the experience, trust, and patience I've needed to truly thrive as a Realtor®.

Finally, to my future clients: I hope and pray this book will help you achieve your homeownership dreams.

Table of Contents

Chapter 4: Working with an Agent.

Chapter 5: Let's Talk Money.

Chapter 6: Interviewing Buyers.

Chapter 7: Congratulations! You Have an Offer!

In Closing.

Lists.

Appendix.

Glossary.

Index.

About the Author: Richard Cordaro

##

Richard Cordaro

Introduction.

Why You Need This Book

You've decided to sell your home. Great! Selling a home is a huge decision and one you likely didn't come to lightly. This is especially true if the home you've decided to sell is your primary residence.

In a nutshell, "The Essential Guide to Selling Your Home: How to Sell Your Home for the Most Amount of Money in the Shortest Amount of Time!" is intended to teach you the basics of the sales process as well as offer some tricks of the trade that can help you get the greatest financial return on your property's sale.

Even if you've sold property before, remember that real estate is a fluid market: trends, laws, sales patterns, and other factors are constantly fluxing and changing. This book offers insight on these latest home selling and home buyer trends.

In addition, "The Essential Guide to Selling Your Home" will refresh your memory about how things generally progress from listing through to sale and beyond because I know that, whether you've been through the selling process before or not, it's nice to have a little help along the way.

What This Book DOESN'T Discuss

I'll be straightforward here:

This book does NOT discuss housing code, **building code**, safety code… basically, any kind of code enforcement. Codes differ from state to state, city to city, township to township, so all I'll say is this: Check with your local authorities on these regulations.

Likewise, I will NOT be informing you which construction and building permits you'll need in order to legally conduct pre-sale renovations on your property. Again, those differ by location, so check with your local authorities.

Finally, this book will NOT be giving you details on how to be a **For Sale by Owner (FSBO)** seller. I get it: Homeowners are generally hands-on people – they've become accustomed to managing their home, taking care of it, perhaps even involving themselves directly in some DIY improvements and projects. Go-getter homeowners are easily enticed by the glamourized idea of selling themselves, thinking it'll save them money (or make them more of it), and that it'll be an easy process. That's why I discuss this topic in Chapter 4: Other than showing you how FSBO sellers do not get more money out of their sales than agent-partnered sellers, I'll say now that you'll miss out on a lot of benefits you get by teaming with a **real estate agent** or **Realtor®**.

In short, if you're certain you want to sell your home yourself there are plenty of books for you out there. However, this isn't one of them.

How to Use This Book

If you purchased a paperback copy of "The Essential Guide to Selling Your Home" you may have noticed that it's fairly compact, unlike similar real estate reference and guidebooks.

At around 200 pages and cut to an easy-to-carry half-letter trim, this book is specifically sized so you can take it with you and find the information you need quickly, like when you're searching for a real estate agent, filling a cart full of DIY home improvement supplies, or doing a walk-through of your home.

Here are other ways this book is designed to help you:

- <u>Special graphics</u> point out tips, tricks, and other information you'll find handy (check out the table of those icons at the end of this chapter);

- <u>Bold text</u> indicates words and terms that are defined in the Glossary. Or, if you're looking for particular information about a topic, simply flip through the Index to locate the applicable page(s);

- <u>A dashed line</u> on the inside of the page indicates worksheets or other guides you can complete and cut out for future reference;

- <u>A double hash (##)</u> means you've come to the end of a chapter; and

- <u>Lined pages</u> are included at the end of every chapter so you can make notations at your leisure.

Of course, I encourage you to read this book from front to back and not just locate the information in it piecemeal. There may be lingering details that you'll miss out on otherwise. But, I get it! Sometimes there's just no time. That's why we created an index, after all: so you can flip to the page you need information from straightaway!

Alright. Now that you've got the gist of how this book works and how to navigate it more easily, let's get down to business and talk about selling your property.

##

Index of Special Markers

ICON	DESCRIPTION
TIPS	The **Tips Jar** will point out money-saving and money-making tips.
Seller's Secrets	**Seller's Secrets** won't necessarily save you money, but may save time or offer quick sale hints.
	Reminders help you remember key tasks and are sometimes partnered with short checklists or other tools.
STORY BOX	**Story Boxes** tell real-life scenarios that showcase a selling concept.
BUYER'S TIP...	If you're selling now, you'll likely be buying soon, too. **Buyer's Tips** relate to a covered topic but from the buyer's perspective.

Table 1: Index of Special Markers

Notes

Chapter 1

Why Are You Selling?

Different Reasons, Terms, & Timelines

Everyone has a different reason for selling their home. Whether it's a new job, marriage, a growing family, or simply wanting a change, each scenario involves varying degrees of the same questions. Namely,

1. How quickly do I need to get out?
2. Why do I need to move?
3. Can I afford to move?
4. Is my property in sellable condition?
5. Should I sell or just rent?

Let's go over these questions individually so you can get a better understanding of how you ought to consider and answer each of them according to your own needs.

How Quickly Do I Need to Get Out?

Everyone's timeline is different. Many times selling a home is an optional choice; sometimes, though, putting a property up for sale is a more urgent matter, for example if someone needs to sell and relocate in order to take care of an ill family member or start a new job.

Whether selling your property is optional or a necessity, you don't want to dally. In real estate, the longer a property sits in a **multiple listing service (MLS)**—a marketing database set up by a group of cooperating real estate brokers—the harder it becomes to sell. Even in a fast-moving market, if a home is listed for too long it goes "stale" and buyers assume something must be wrong with it, in which case they'll pass it up for a "fresher" listing.

That's why I strongly suggest you and your real estate agent work out a plan to reduce the price of your listing at 30, 60, and 90 days in.[†] Figure out by what amounts you want to reduce prices now—before the listing goes live—so you won't have to spend valuable time figuring out those details as each day grows more and more crucial. By using this price reduction technique, the number of days your listing is on the market will be minimized and buyer interest will be maintained.

Also within the timing construct there are certain categories of seller that you should watch out for. Do you know what kind of seller YOU are? If not, indicate which of the following statements resonate most with you.

☐ A: "I need out… now!"

☐ B: "I'm in no hurry, but now would be nice."

☐ C: "I'm selling an investment property, so profit is more important to me than saving time, but I do want to sell soon."

☐ D: "I have all the time in the world. I could sell or not; it doesn't matter to me."

Why Do I Need to Move?

The "why" to your need matters a great deal. Knowing the reason or reasons why you want to sell your property can help you determine if selling really is the right choice for you.

If you answered A above—"I need out… now!"—ask yourself, "Why now?"

[†]   Take a look in the Appendix at the 30-60-90-Day Price Change Schedule instructions and accompanying template.

- Has your financial status changed so that you can no longer afford your mortgage payments?

- Do you need to relocate due to another obligation (e.g. work, family) and you need the cash from your property's sale to purchase a home elsewhere?

- Are you simply bored of the area (Ex: You don't like your neighbors, your town, or are just seeking a new environment)?

- Have you and your family outgrown your current home?

Any of the above reasons (or another) could have been well thought out or it could be a spur-of-the-moment decision. Understand your own motives, because you don't want to rush into offloading your property on the chance you might miss living where you are now and regret selling, especially if other solutions exist to solve your "why" reason.

For instance, maybe you like where you live and like your home but you're just looking for a change. In that case, you could opt to purchase (or rent) a second home elsewhere to give yourself the variety you seek without having to sacrifice this current property.

Or maybe you love where you live but your family has simply outgrown the house you're in. In that case, have you considered hiring a contractor or home designer to go over options for renovating your current property? Much can be done to improve the use of space in homes, especially older ones, so selling isn't always the only option. It is possible to keep your neighborhood, your home, and still have space for your growing family to thrive!

If you still think selling is the right choice and you've thought everything through, contact a real estate agent and tell them you need to sell, ASAP, and hand them a copy of the 30-60-90-day worksheet so they can use it to help speed up the sale of your home.

If you answered B or C—you're in no rush but selling as soon as possible would be convenient—then the **30-60-90-Day Price Change Schedule** is perfect for you, too. You're likely willing to give a little on your price in order to save some time as long as it results in a fair to good profit.

If you answered D, the price reduction worksheet probably won't be much use to you since you're looking at maximizing your profit and don't care how long it takes to get it. You may be willing to sit on your listing for months (or years) and not feel a need to drop the price to get a quicker sale, and that's fine. But, as a courtesy, please let your real estate agent know this is the type of seller you are: That you're in no hurry and that you won't reduce the listing price no matter how long the listing sits. This way they won't spin their wheels (and lose their sanity) finding and showing your home to buyers who aren't willing to pay full price.

Whatever your reason or whatever type of seller you are, the point is to have thought through the decision to sell and that it isn't an impulsive choice that you may later regret.

Can I Afford to Move?

Sometimes selling a home seems profitable, but there

are costs you'll incur both before and after the sale has concluded. For example:

- Costs to update or renovate prior to selling;
- Closing costs (including **earnest money**);
- The expense of relocating you, your family, and all your stuff;
- The remaining mortgage balance on your home.

Is My Property in Sellable Condition?

Buyers obviously expect lived-in homes to be, well, *lived in*, and that includes a few bumps and bruises to the interior or exterior. However, few buyers want to purchase a *true* fixer-upper—you know, a home with torn carpeting, missing or cracked tiles, out-of-date guts (e.g. electrical, plumbing, insulation, appliances), or worse. Also, fixer-uppers are more difficult to sell for a premium price since buyers in that market either can't afford anything else or intend to flip the property for profit. Hence, they'll more likely low-ball on price and more strenuously negotiate due to real or perceived condition issues (e.g. ones that potential buyers say they'll "have to fix," even if inspectors say everything checks out).

So, the question "Is my property in sellable condition?" is dependent on what kind of timeline you're looking at for selling your property and what kind of number you expect to get from the sale.

Don't get me wrong: It is possible to get the most amount of money in a short amount of time for a fixer-upper. You just need to realize that that amount of money and that amount of time will be likely lower and higher, respectively, than with a home that is turnkey or move-in ready.

Closely related to the condition question is question #1 ("Can I Afford to Move?"). The affordability question needs to involve considerations for investments into your current property, pre-listing. That is, you need to consider the money you'll likely spend on both required (e.g. code violations or lender demanded) and optional improvements that will help you sell your home more quickly.

Should I Sell or Just Rent?

If you're sure that staying in your current home just won't do, there are two ways for you to get out: sell or rent.

Selling isn't always the best answer, as renting your home can offer some benefits, especially if there's no absolute need to rid yourself of your current property right away.

Renting makes sense if you're able to:

(a) Charge enough rent to cover your mortgage payment plus some, OR

(b) You have no mortgage, so all rental income will go directly in your pocket; AND

(c) You have an interest in either maintaining an investment property or may want to move back into your old home in the future.

Rental income is nice as long as the benefits outweigh the cons. You can be your own rental agent or hire a management agency to find and handle renters for you. More importantly: Are you looking for profit, or would you be happy breaking even?

Deciding whether to sell or rent also depends on how FAST you need out of your home. Setting up a rental doesn't take as long but you may not then have the funds to purchase another residence (if you need somewhere to go/selling your primary), but getting out of the responsibility of your property clean via a sale can be less hassle in the long-run.

Overall, meeting with a trustworthy real estate agent to discuss these questions is my best suggestion. They'll offer insight on the current market, help you dig deeper to determine where you fall in the spectrum of answers to the sell versus rent question, and be able to tell you what, if anything, your property needs to rise to sellable (or rentable) condition.

##

Notes

Chapter 2

When Are You Selling?

Determining Your Area's Selling Season

In addition to helping you answer the questions posed in the previous chapter, another thing a real estate agent can offer is his or her insight into when the best time is to list your property.

If you're in the "I need out, now!" boat, it likely doesn't matter when your area's **selling season** is; you're going to list it immediately regardless of which month you're starting out in.

If you're more flexible in your timing, you may find you have a few months or longer to do renovations and updates before the selling season arrives. This is great news, as it enables you to stress less about timelines and really focus on doing everything you possibly can to get the most money from the sale of your home during the best possible time of year.

What Affects Selling Seasons?

Home sales follow general seasonal trends that are very similar to the timing trends in the auto industry. Homes and cars are both large purchases and smart consumers invest a lot of thought, energy, and legwork into making a decision on a vehicle or home. Those who pay very close attention to these markets are able to recognize real-life associations between the two, as home and auto sales are both strong indicators of the economy and tend to change in step with one another according to consumer confidence.

Just like a potential buyer will spend hours researching the car that's just right for them—from vehicle histories to mechanical inspections—so they will spend hours researching for their new home. And, just like a potential buyer will spend lots of energy and driving around to physically look at and test drive all those different cars, so they will for their new home.

I make this comparison because not everyone has sold a home but most people have purchased a car. Considering your buyer from a car purchasing perspective can help you get out of your own head and adopt a helpful understanding of the buyer's viewpoint. Selling a home isn't only about making your house pretty and staking a sign in the yard on the right day: It's a lot to do with understanding home shoppers on both a broad and specific level.

(Please don't get overwhelmed! We'll more thoroughly cover the buyers' mindset in Chapter 3 and Chapter 6, so we won't spend a whole lot of time on those concepts here.)

There are two types of factors that affect a selling season: predictable and unpredictable.

Predictable factors include weather, societal activity (e.g. holidays), and family status (e.g. single, married, with children) and how that status affects buyers' activity (e.g. the impact of school-aged children on a buyer's needs and desires).

Unpredictable factors include things like demographics, mortgage interest rates, and housing supply and demand in your area.

Unpredictable factors are very much just that: unpredictable. While we may hear chatter of an upcoming change to mortgage interest rates, very often nobody knows what'll happen to interest until—BAM—it's happened. Until then, it's anyone's guess.

That's why we'll focus on Predictable Factors, things you can rely on in order to decide when the optimal time is to list your home to get the most money.

Weather

Like in the auto sales industry, weather makes a big difference to an area's selling season. For example, home sales drop dramatically in the American northeast in the dead of winter when it's too cold for most people to want to go out and view homes, and in the Southwest in the peak of summer when it's equally too hot.

As a general rule, spring through summer is prime time to have your home for sale. The busyness of the holidays is concluded; families with children don't worry so much about school and therefore moving is less strenuous. Consider having your home ready to be listed around April or May so it can be shown at the peak of the selling season. That means you'll need to plan to finish any renovations long before then.

Societal Activity

It's easy to predict what society is up to: Just look at a calendar! Things like holidays and school schedules can impact buyers' ability and willingness to get out and look at homes.

Family Status

Single individuals or couples generally have more flexibility in regard to when they're able to buy a house (for instance, they're schedules aren't dictated by school calendars). This means that they're under less pressure to buy during the busy season and will often have more time to spare to negotiate and really shop around.

Families with school-aged children, however, are generally more likely to find, purchase, and move into a home at the end or outside of the school year (that is, during the selling season). This schedule can vary depending on whether the buyer's children and/or your home's school district follow a traditional or year-round calendar.[†]

##

[†] A special note on family status: According to the Fair Housing Act of 1968, you cannot refuse to sell or rent a dwelling to any person because of race, color, religion, sex, familial status, or national origin. This is a Federal Law and as such extends over state lines. If you discriminate against a buyer for any of these protected statuses you could have a filing put against you which could result in legal action. Employment also falls under this status umbrella, as a buyer's work schedule may strongly dictate when they'll be able to view a home and, in later dealings, respond to inquiries, sign paperwork, and attend to other needs in the process of purchasing a home.

Being sure you're adhering to this and other federal and state laws is just one more reason to hire a licensed real estate agent to help you with the sale of your home.

Notes

WORKSHEET A
The Seller's Why, When, & How

This worksheet will help determine if selling your home is the right decision for you. If it is, this worksheet can also help you prepare as you move forward toward listing.

. . .

1. Why do you feel you need to move?

☐ A: "My financial status has changed and I can no longer afford my mortgage payments."

☐ B: "I need to relocate due to an obligation (e.g. work, family) and need the cash from my property's sale to purchase another home or to cover moving expenses."

☐ C: "I'm bored of my area (e.g. I don't like my neighbors, my town, or am just seeking a new environment)."

☐ D: "My family and I have outgrown our current home."

☐ E: "It's another reason not mentioned here."

- *If you chose A or B, there's no question: You have to move! But does that mean you need to* sell*? Consider this as you proceed to Question #2...*

- *If you chose C, try re-engaging with your current community through activities and new experiences, or consider renovating your home to renew your interest in it. If these solutions don't help, then perhaps moving*

WORKSHEET A continued

is the best option for you after all.

- *If you chose D, try consulting with a contractor or home design specialist to discuss ways you can expand your current space. This is an especially appealing option if you like your community and don't necessarily want to move. If renovating isn't possible, selling your current property in order to purchase a larger home may be your best bet.*

- *If you chose E, just remember that selling isn't always the right choice. Talk to friends and family, or consult with a real estate agent to discuss the best option(s) for your particular situation before you sell and possibly regret the decision later.*

2. Can you afford to move?

☐ A: "I can afford to move whether or not my property sells."

☐ B: "I don't know."

☐ C: "I will not be able to move unless I sell (or rent) my property first."

- *If you chose A, you have the option of being pickier about offers that come in on your home in order to maximize your profit. However, time is money, so being too picky can result in lost profit! This topic is covered more in Chapter 5.*

- *If you chose B, I'd suggest using a moving cost calculator to help determine how much of a relocating expense you should expect. These calculators can be found in*

WORKSHEET A *continued*

abundance on the Internet.

- *If you chose C, you're obviously under stress to list and sell (and then perhaps buy!) as quickly as possible. Pay close attention to tips on staging your home and listing prices.*

3. Should you sell, or would renting out your home be the better choice?

- If you answered A or B to Question #1, <u>selling is for you!</u> *Skip Question #4; proceed to Question #5.*

- If you answered C to Question #1 and re-engaging or renovating won't solve your core issue, then <u>selling is a good option for you, but renting is not out of the question.</u> Consider talking with a real estate agent or property management company about the benefits of renting out your home. *Proceed to Question #4.*

- If you answerd D to Question #1 and renovating isn't a reasonable solution for you, then <u>selling is likely your best option, though renting out your current home for additional income may be beneficial since you still like the area.</u> I'd suggest consulting with a real estate agent about the benefits of renting out your current property. *Proceed to Question #4*

- If you answered E to Question #1, again I suggest you consult with a real estate agent to get their take on whether selling or renting out your home is best for your situation. *Proceed to Question #4.*

WORKSHEET A *continued*

4. Have you consulted with a real estate agent or property management company about your home and the current rental market?

☐ A: "No, I haven't because I'm not interested in renting my property even if it is a viable option." *Proceed to Question #5.*

☐ B: "Yes, I have, but the rent collected would not be worth the trouble." *Proceed to Question #5.*

☐ C: "Yes, I have. It has been determined that rent collected may or will provide enough income to be worth keeping my property." *Congratulations on your potential as an investment property owner! However, I encourage you to continue with the rest of this worksheet in case you're still considering selling.*

5. How quickly do you need to sell your current home?

☐ A: "I need out... now!"

☐ B: "I'm in no hurry, but now would be nice."

☐ C: "I'm selling an investment property, so profit is more important to me than saving time, but sooner would be better."

☐ D: "I have all the time in the world."

- *If you chose A, this book is exactly what you need! Pay special attention to details about prepping your home for the best showings possible and quick-sale tactics — like the Price Reduction Schedule — to close the sale of your home ASAP.*

WORKSHEET A *continued*

- *If you chose B or C, this book will certainly come in handy. Pay attention to tips on accepting offers, though. Because you have a little extra time on your side, you may be able to be pickier about accepting (or denying) offers that come in that aren't quite the amount you're hoping for.*

- *If you chose D, this book will offer some help, but you are certainly not under stress to sell right away. The time-saving tips will be less applicable to you than money-maximizing tips like those discussed in Chapter 5, "Let's Talk Money".*

6. Have you considered all financial costs of selling, including renovation, repurchase, and relocation?

☐ If YES, you probably won't have many surprises in store as you move forward with your sale. You know how much you need to keep available to move and, therefore, how much you can spend on renovations.

☐ If NO, I suggest using a Moving Cost Calculator to determine how much you'll need to keep handy to cover relocation expenses. Also, pay special attention to Chapter 3 ("Fix It") and take many notes: Doing so will help you determine how much renovations and/or fixes will cost for your home, pre-listing, and will therefore help you get a better feel for the total cost of selling your home.

7. Is your property in sellable condition?

☐ A: "Yes—I have consulted with a real estate agent and they have determined my property is in sellable condition." *Skip Questions #8 and #9; proceed to #10.*

WORKSHEET A *continued*

□ B: "Yes—I have *not* consulted with a real estate agent, but I have determined on my own that my property is in sellable condition."

□ C: "I don't know." *Go to Question #8.*

□ D: "No—I have consulted with a real estate agent and they have determined my property is *not* in sellable condition." *Go to Question #9.*

□ E: "No—I have *not* consulted with a real estate agent but have determined on my own that my property is *not* in sellable condition." *Go to Question #9.*

8. If you are unsure about the condition of your property, are you willing to consult with a real estate agent to determine its sellability?

□ A: "Yes—I am willing to consult with a real estate agent about the condition of my property."

□ B: "No—I am not interested in working with an agent to sell my home."

- *If you chose A above, please proceed to Question #9.*

- *If you chose B, be aware that you will likely not get the most money for your property, nor is it likely that you will be able to sell your property in the shortest time possible. That said, it may be best for you to reconsider if selling is really the right move for you at this point in time. Proceed to Question #9.*

WORKSHEET A *continued*

9. Are you able to fund renovations and fixes on your property that are *required to bring it to sellable condition?* (This does not mean *optional* renovations and fixes to increase value and sale price, but rather those that would be required by law, lender, or building code.)

- ☐ If YES, that's excellent! *Proceed to Question #10.*
- ☐ If NO, consider these options:
  1. Discuss with a real estate agent the possibility of listing your property "As Is".
  2. Consult with a lender about lines of credit you can use toward home improvement.

10. Have you consulted with a real estate agent about renovations and fixes that will improve your chances of increasing your properties asking price?

☐ YES: Great! *Proceed to Question #11.*

☐ NO: Obviously it's not necessary to get permission from an agent to make improvements on your own home, but keep in mind that few people know what renovations attract buyers the way real estate agents do. Consider getting an agent's opinion before spending time and money—or, likewise, wasting it—on improvements. *Proceed to Question #11.*

WORKSHEET A continued

Calculating & Determining Important Dates

11. When is your area's selling season?

From ___*month*___ to ___*month*___ .

12. According to this selling season, when do you want your property to be listed?

I want my property listed by ___*MM / DD / YYYY*___ .

This is your Desired Listing Date:

_____

13. To achieve the chosen listing date, renovations and/or fixes need to be completed by:

___*Date from #12*___ - 2 weeks[†] = ___*MM / DD / YYYY*___

14. How will I complete my renovations/fixes?

☐ A: "I will be doing *all* the renovation work myself."

☐ B: "I will do *some* of the renovation/fix work myself and hire out to professionals for the rest."

☐ C: "I will be relying completely on professional contractors and handymen to complete my projects."

• *If you chose B or C, consider tapping into a real estate*

† Why a two-week gap? Giving yourself two weeks between the final day of renovations and the listing date creates a cushion of time for you to handle any incidental or unexpected situations with minimal rush.

WORKSHEET A *continued*

agent as a resource for reliable contractors and handymen in your area. They may be able to point you toward professionals who are well versed in conducting home renovations in preparation for listing and sale.

15. How long do I estimate renovations/fixes to take?

I estimate all projects to take ___#___ weeks to complete.

16. In order have the property ready for listing by the date determined in #11, I need to BEGIN renovations and/or fixes by...

Using a calendar, count backward *#15 answer* weeks from ___*Answer from #13*___...

This is your Renovation Start Date:
___*MM / DD / YYYY*___

17. Are you able to begin renovations on the calculated start date?

☐ YES: Great! It looks like you're ready to read the rest of this book. Don't forget to mark your calendar with these important dates, and keep the answers you've selected on this worksheet in mind as you proceed through your preparations to sell your home.

☐ NO: Don't worry. It's common for renovation timelines not to line up with a desired listing date. Consider these options to fix the problem:

1. Add another week or two to your projects'

WORKSHEET A continued

incidental cushion. Adding more time won't necessarily hurt you, but lessening or removing the cushion could.

2. If you're unable to begin renovations due to financial delays (e.g. waiting for approval on a home improvement line of credit)...

    *   See if there are projects on your list that are low- to no-cost that you can handle in the meantime.
    *   Talk with contractors about establishing a payment plan that will make your projects more affordable.

3. Reduce the number of projects on your list in order to shorten the renovation completion time (see Question #15).

4. Change your desired listing date so that the Renovation Start Date is more suitable to your situation.

. . .

This is the end of Worksheet A.

Additional "Worksheet A" Notes

Chapter 3

Fix It.

Now that you've decided that selling is, in fact, the right decision for you, it's time to take a step back and assess the condition of your property.

This step involves getting (or not getting) pre-listing inspections, making lists of what to **fix** or **renovate**, deciding who and how to do those tasks, and other considerations.

Your Home Isn't Perfect: Pre-Listing Inspections

Obtaining a home **inspection** is a no-brainer and often a requirement of the sale (e.g. the buyer's mortgage lender requires an inspection to make certain of the condition and current market value of the property their money is being invested into).

The real question is whether you, the seller, want to wait to inspect when you're days or weeks vested into the sales process with a buyer or if you want to cut to the chase and lay all your cards on the table in the beginning.

Waiting has its advantages. If you're well into negotiations with the buyer chances are, unless you offered to pay for the inspections as an incentive (there's a section on **buyer incentives** in Chapter 5), the buyer will pay for the inspection. That's one less expense for you.

But waiting also has its disadvantages. The inspection could reveal a flaw that you weren't aware needed fixing and therefore aren't prepared to mend. This could be a distasteful enough surprise to the buyer that it causes them to change their offer, demand fixes prior to purchase, or back out of the deal altogether.

More pros and cons of offering a pre-listing inspection can be viewed on the next page.

Pre-sale inspections' benefits outweigh the disadvantages, which is why I recommend having them done. Though there will be a monetary cost to you for having a licensed and/or nationally certified professional inspect your home, the fact that the property has already been looked over offers both you and any potential buyers' that much more peace of mind.

DIY vs. Professional Inspections

You could, of course, opt to inspect your home yourself and save from paying someone else to do it for you. Just know that a DIY inspection won't carry weight with lenders or banks who may require the assurance of a licensed home inspector's trained eye, and your report may not impress buyers who may feel your "findings" are too biased to be of any real value.

Instead of a legal document, think of your DIY inspection report as a formal FYI. You're simply making it known that you're aware your house isn't perfect and are willing to accept there are or could be issues with the property and that you're willing to work with buyers to come to some agreement about fixing said issues.

Honesty in real estate goes a long way. Everyone knows no property is perfect, yet some homeowners still go out of their way to up-sell, describing nothing except the positive aspects of the listing and excluding any realistic downsides. To the realistic buyer, a sparkling five-star review simply won't be trusted and they'll be left feeling like you may be trying too hard to impress them in order to sell them a lemon or money pit.

It's difficult to be unbiased about what belongs to us. This includes our houses. After all, we've poured money,

Getting a Pre-Listing Home Inspection	
PROS	**CONS**
Fewer surprises for both seller and buyer.	You'll have to shell out about $200-$500.
You'll have time to fix issues before they have a chance to delay your sale.	You may have to fix (i.e. spend money on) things you otherwise wouldn't.
You could save money (and time) in the long run.	You could be legally obligated to disclose problems you otherwise wouldn't.
Early detection of issues could lead to a faster close.	Revealed problems could delay closing until those items are fixed.
You're showing a good faith effort and buyers will know you're willing to go beyond what's expected.	Buyers could take advantage of your good faith efforts and ask you to do even more.
You could avoid repeating repairs (once during renovation and again post-inspection) if you find out the renovated fix was not to code.	If you intend to sell your home as a fixer-upper, a pre-inspection becomes less valuable during negotiations.
Your home's assets are easier to highlight.	Your home's defects are easier to highlight.

Table 2: Getting a Pre-Listing Home Inspection

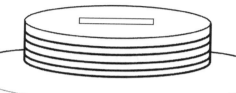

TIPS

A Warning About Talking Up Your Home

It's natural to want to up-talk your home to make the sale, but be sure you don't go too far in the other direction either. In an effort to be objective you could say too much about your home's problems and talk potential buyers away by unintentionally devaluing your property.

It's safer to let your real estate agent do the talking to buyers and their agents.

time, and sweat into our homes! As a result, it's easy to overlook problems or inflate assets. That's why I recommend hiring a licensed professional to take care of your pre-listing inspection for you.

However, if you insist on doing a DIY inspection report, be sure the results of your inspection are concise, objective, and realistic. Perhaps consider having a friend or your agent look over the analysis to catch any remarks that could appear biased or untrustworthy. (I've created a worksheet in the Appendix that you can use as a template for the formal report you offer to potential buyers.)

Determining Your Target Buyers

Before you do anything—before you renovate, before you hire a home inspector, before you even talk with a real estate agent—you should consider who your target buyer is. That is: What type of person are you trying to sell to?

Why is this important?

Well, there are two reasons: First, you need to get an idea of when your buyers will be in the market. This goes back to determining your area's selling season and who will likely be looking at houses when.

If you know when the best time is to put your home up for sale you'll have the best opportunity to beat the competition into the marketplace, making your home one of the first available for buyers to see.

Second, different types of buyers expect different things out of a home. For instance, a **turn-key** buyer is looking for a home where everything is finished and is also likely to be expecting the home to be updated and/or modernized, while someone seeking a **fixer-upper** property can generally do without bells and whistles and will even want portions of a home to be in need of repair.

So, what does your ideal buyer look like?

Though you're not legally allowed to discriminate, it still helps to get an idea of what house hunters in your area expect in general *as well as* what type(s) of house hunters a property like yours will attract.

This mentality of determining target buyers is little more than what salespeople everywhere call Targeted Marketing.

In sales, a target market is the market (i.e. the population) a company wants to sell its products and services to. **Targeted Marketing** is just a fancy way of saying you're

Seller's Secrets

Beware Hidden Discoloration

Paint and wallpaper can discolor or fade from exposure to light and air.

Remove art, decor, and picture frames from walls and see if the color beneath them differs from the rest of the room. If so, it's time to repaint, because when you move out those discolored areas will show prominently in the absence of your wall art, and the buyer may come back to you with a complaint.

focusing (targeting) your marketing (sales) efforts toward a certain audience, specifically buyers whose needs and desires most closely match your product's (in this case, your home's) qualities and assets. For instance, if your home is close to a school, you may focus your marketing efforts on families with children. On the other hand, if you're selling property in an urban high rise, you may decide to focus on attracting attention from singles or business people.

Choosing a target market population provides direction to your sales activities, including but not limited to activities like:

- *What* features of the home you decide to spend money on fixing or renovating;
- *Where* and *how* you and your real estate agent advertise; and
- *When* target buyers will be shopping so you can list at the most appropriate time.

Identifying your target market is an essential step in developing a plan to get the most money from the sale of your home.

Your Walk-Through: How to Decide What Should Be Fixed and What Shouldn't Be

Whether or not you decide to get a professional inspection done before you list, it's still a good idea to go through your house room by room and make note of any condition issues or potential problems that could affect your property's listing price, value, and show-ability.

Here's a basic rundown of the sort of things you should be looking for as you walk through your home:

- Damage;
- Chipping paint;
- Code violations[†];
- Safety or condition issues (e.g. loose stair rails, peeling or moldy tile caulking);
- Out-of-date fixtures and features (e.g. shag carpeting, checkerboard parquet flooring);
- Faded or discolored paint or wallpaper;
- Unique styles and features specific to you and your family (e.g. character decals on the walls of a child's bedroom);
- Clutter (this doesn't only mean too many knick-knacks, but also over-furnished rooms or walls overrun with too much art or picture frames).

In the pages following this section you'll find a worksheet that will help you organize your thoughts and findings during your **walk-through**. Just remember: This walk-through isn't the same as your **pre-listing inspection**! A walk-through is an informal exercise to help you to determine which items you'll consider fixing or renovating prior to listing your home for sale; a pre-listing inspection is a more thorough inspection done by either you (the homeowner) or a licensed home inspector and is usually followed by a written report that's made available to real estate agents and potential buyers as a reference.

Keep in mind the worksheet is intentionally generic. It's based on a fairly standard three-bedroom, two-bath, two-story home. Your house likely has a different num-

---

† Consult with your local code enforcement agency or with a licensed home inspector to be assured your home is to code.

Some Homes Need TLC Before Listing

I was asked to look at a home that the owners had trouble selling. It had been rented out and was in need of some TLC. Listing agents before me failed to recommend that things be done to make the home appealing to buyers.

Selling a home is a competition. Buyers are comparing your home with others they see, so it needs to have a better appearance and value than the competition.

There are three things to remember in real estate: Price, Location, and Condition. Location couldn't be changed, but price and condition could.

This home needed to be painted inside, have the carpets cleaned, and get landscaping done. We were able to improve the appearance and curb appeal of the home dramatically and sold it for the price the seller wanted. A happy ending for all!

ber and type of rooms, or different features in each room – or even different features on its exterior – that are not listed. In such cases, use the "Other" spaces to make your own notes, or extend your notetaking to the *Notes* section at the end of this chapter.

DIY, Handyman, or Contractor?

Like with getting a pre-listing inspection, you have the choice between doing it yourself (**DIY**) or hiring out when it comes to doing the hands-on work.

While being a DIY homeowner is admirable, there is such a thing as getting too ambitious when it comes to taking on fix-it projects solo. DIY-ing is great for simple repairs or upgrades that won't require inspections, permits, special tools, or heavy equipment. The things that fall into these categories are typically small and cosmetic. Think replacing faucets, painting walls, or hanging curtains.

If you're a seasoned homeowner or a handy sort of person, you may find my suggestion of sticking to small handyman-type projects to be an insult to your abilities. But, please, let me explain:

Fixing things in your soon-to-be-listed home isn't merely a question of 'Can you do it yourself?' but also a question of time and money.

Remember, you don't merely have to go through a run-of-the-mill honey-do list. There isn't time to linger because you need to get your home listed by a certain time (the selling season) and that puts a lot of limits and constraints on how long you have to get things done, and done right.

And it's not only about how fast you can work, but

Seller's Secrets

Appliances & Furniture: Keep It Clean

Some sellers choose to leave some or all appliances and furnishings – like bedroom sets, pool tables, or window treatments – behind for the new owners. In some states, that these items stay with the house is an assumed part of any home purchase. In others, they're perhaps included as part of negotiations. Either way, if you leave any appliances or furnishings behind it's smart to assess their condition.

Consider professionally cleaning or updating items you'll be leaving with the home, like getting older furniture reupholstered or appliances deep cleaned or serviced, so it doesn't seem like you're just leaving your old junk behind to the new owners

also about how much time you'll need to get construction inspectors and code enforcement officers to your site to sign off on any big jobs. In many instances, you cannot move forward with construction until you have the all-clear from the authorities and, depending on how busy the inspectors' schedules are, you may be waiting days or weeks to get them to approve your work.

You also likely have a day job that you need to go to; you don't have all day, every day, to spend working on fixing your home. And you might not have the financial

WORKSHEET B
Walk-Through Checklist

Part 1: Interior

Bedrooms

MASTER	Good ✓	Needs Work ✗
Ceiling Fan		
Closet		
...Rods		
...Shelving		
Electrical		
...Lighting (permanent)		
...Outlets		
...Switches		
Flooring		
Walls		
Windows & Doors		
Other: _____		
Other: _____		

BEDROOM #2	Good ✓	Needs Work ✗
Ceiling Fan		
Closet		
...*Rods*		
...*Shelving*		
Electrical		
...*Lighting (permanent)*		
...*Outlets*		
...*Switches*		
Flooring		
Walls		
Windows & Doors		
Other: _____		
Other: _____		

BEDROOM #3	Good ✓	Needs Work ✗
Ceiling Fan		
Closet		
...*Rods*		
...*Shelving*		

Electrical		
...Lighting (permanent)		
...Outlets		
...Switches		
Flooring		
Walls		
Windows & Doors		
Other: _____		
Other: _____		

Kitchen, Baths, and Utility Rooms

	Mark if the item shows problems.			
PLUMBING & WATER	Kitchen	Bath 1	Bath 2	Utility
Hardware				
...Drain (sink)				
...Drain (tub)				
...Faucet (sink)				
...Faucet (tub)				
...Showerhead				
...Other: _____				
...Other: _____				

Pipes (under sink)				
...*Active dripping*				
...*Corrosion/Rust*				
...*Water damage*				
...*Other:* _____				
Toilet				
...*Bowl*				
...*Tank*				
...*Other:* _____				
Other: _____				
Other: _____				

Electric

OUTLETS	*Mark if the item shows problems.*			
	Kitchen	Bath 1	Bath 2	Utility
Outlets				
...*Damaged or missing covers*				
...*Non-functional*				
...*Other:* _____				
Switches				
...*Damaged or missing covers*				
...*Non-functional*				
...*Other:* _____				
Other: _____				
Other: _____				

Living Spaces

Mark if the item shows problems.

	Entry	Hall	Living	Kitchen
Baseboards				
Built-in Shelving				
Ceiling Fans				
Crown Moulding				
Fireplace				
...Firebox				
...Hearth				
...Mantle				
...Surround				
Flooring				
...Broken planks or tiles				
...Needs cleaning				
...Peeling/Scuffs/Tears				
...Other: _____				
Walls (paint, dents, etc.)				
Windows & Doors				
...Frames				
...Glass				
...Hinges, Latches, or Locks				
Other: _____				
Other: _____				

Other Areas

GARAGE	Good ✓	Needs Work ✗
Doors		
...*Exterior Access (yard to garage)*		
...*Garage Door (main)*		
...*Interior Access (house to garage)*		
Floor		
Lighting		
Outlets & Switches		
Permanent Fixtures (*e.g. shelves, workbenches, tool racks*)		
Walls		
Windows		
Other: _____		
Other: _____		

STAIRS	Good ✓	Needs Work ✗
Flooring		
Railing		
...*Damaged or Loose*		
...*Not to Code*		
...*Other:* _____		
Walls *(paint, scuffs, holes, etc.)*		
Other: _____		
Other: _____		

BASEMENT	Good ✓	Needs Work ✗
Door *(exterior)*		
Door *(interior)*		
Electrical		
...*Lighting*		
...*Outlets*		
...*Switches*		
...*Other:* _____		
Floor		
Stairs		

Walls		
Windows		
Other: _____		
Other: _____		

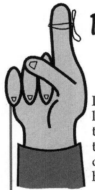

REMINDER...

Check for Compliance with the Latest Building Codes

If you're planning on fixing your home prior to listing, remember to have an inspector come in to look around. Especially if your home is older, there may be some things that are no longer compliant that may need adjusting before your home will pass a buyer's or lender's inspection.

For example, older homes may have stair railings that were to code when they were built but are no longer. In many places years ago, spaces between railings were allowed to be much wider than current safety codes require so that small children cannot fall through.

These are the sorts of details a home inspector will be able to point out with a quick look around.

Walk-Through Checklist

Part 2: Exterior

HARD *(Permanent)* FEATURES	Good ✓	Needs Work ✗
Chimneys		
Deck(s)		
Doors		
...Front (Main)		
...Back #1		
...Back #2		
...Other: _____		
Driveway		
Electrical		
...Light Fixture(s)		
...Outlets		
...Other: _____		
Fencing & Gates		
Faucets & Hoses		
Gutters		
Outbuildings & Sheds		

Patio(s) & Porches		
Retaining Walls		
Sidewalks & Permanent Walk-ways		
Siding		
Windows		
Other: _____		
Other: _____		
Other: _____		

SOFT *(Nonpermanent)* FEA-TURES	Good ✓	Needs Work ✗
Drainage *(e.g. channels, ditches, French drains)*		
Flowerbeds & Gardens		
...Drainage		
...Mulching		
...Soil		
...Other: _____		
Furniture		
Hanging Pots & Planters		
Lawn		
Lighting *(e.g. solar path lights, string lighting, paper lanterns)*		

Paths & Walkways		
Shrubbery		
Trees: SEE NEXT TABLE	—	—
Other: _____		
Other: _____		

TREE-SPECIFIC QUESTIONS	NO	YES	NOTES...
Any trees that need new soil, mulch, or trimming?			
Any dead trees that need to be removed?			
Any sick or dying trees?			
Any trees too close to...			
...Main Home?			
...Neighboring Properties?			
...Outbuildings?			
...Sidewalks, Driveways, Walkways?			
...Street, Streetlights, Powerlines?			
Any trees currently causing foundation problems?			
Any trees currently causing roof or gutter problems?			
Any low hanging branches that need to be trimmed right away?			

Any branches or roots growing across your property line(s) into neighboring property?			

Tree-Related Notes: _____

_____

_____

_____

_____

Seller's Secrets

Trees Can Add Significant Value

According to some real estate and property appraisal groups, a single healthy, mature tree can add between $1,000-$10,000 to a home's value. Significant, indeed!

Keep trees healthy & properly trimmed — and away from foundations and structures — to add the most value. Hire a professional arborist or a landscaping firm that specializes in trees to come and inspect your trees for pests, disease, or other needs to keep them in tip-top shape.

If you're planning on landscaping to improve curb appeal, consider planting a few trees instead of only opting for the typical flowers, sod, and shrubbery many sellers install to give your property a little extra oomph in the marketplace.

Arbor Day Foundation, "Benefits of Trees". Copyright 2018. URL: www.arborday.org/trees/benefits.cfm. Cited: 26April2018.

Walk-Through Checklist

Part 3: Appliances & Furnishings

Appliances

Environment Control	Stays with Home	Good ✓	Needs Work ✗
Air Conditioning Unit(s) - Permanent	X		
Air Conditioning Unit(s) - Window/Portable			
Air Purifier(s)			
Humidifier(s)			
Space Heater(s)			
Other: _____			
Other: _____			

Laundry Room	Stays with Home	Good ✓	Needs Work ✗
Clothes Rack - Mobile			
Dryer			
Washer			
Other: _____			
Other: _____			

Kitchen	Stays with Home	Good ✓	Needs Work ✗
Dish Washer (*countertop or in-cabinet*)			
Microwave			
Oven/Stove			
Refrigerator			
Toaster Oven			
Utility/Microwave Cart (*mobile*)			
Water Jug Dispenser (*portable*)			
Wine Rack/Cabinet			
Other: _____			
Other: _____			

Other	Stays with Home	Good ✓	Needs Work ✗
Box Fan			
Fire Pit			
Hot Plate			
Mini- or Wine Refrigerator			
Patio Heater(s)			
Other: _____			

Furnishings

	Stays with Home	Good ✓	Needs Work ✗
Bedroom Sets			
...Bedroom 1			
...Bedroom 2			
...Master Bedroom			
...Other (e.g. basement bedroom)			
Bookcase(s)			
China Cabinet/Curio			
Coffee Table(s)			
Desk(s)			
Dining Table & Chairs			
File Cabinet(s)			
Gaming (*e.g. pool table, dartboard, pinball machine*)			
Recliner(s) & Sofa(s)			
Window Treatments			
Other: _____			
Other: _____			

. . .

This is the end of Worksheet B.

BUYER'S TIP ...

Check the Small Stuff

During your tour of a property, take a few moments to look at small maintenance details. For example, check to see that the HVAC filter is reasonably clean; that the whole house water filtration system filter isn't gunked up; or that there isn't excessive calcium buildup on the showerheads.

Though it's never a guarantee of a home's true condition, you can feel reasonably confident that if a homeowner has been diligent about taking care of these smaller items, they've likely taken care of the home's bigger maintenance needs too.

Additional "Worksheet B" Notes

resources to invest in things like tools, supplies, materials, or even fuel to go from the hardware or home improvement store and back to your house again umpteen times, week after week, until the projects are complete.

Ask yourself:

- "How long will it take me to accomplish this list of projects on my own?";
- "How much will it cost me to do it myself?"; AND
- "Can I do this work as well as a professional could?"

These questions are sometimes cast to the wayside in a homeowner's ambitious attempt to do everything DIY right away. The saying "spend a dollar to save a dime" applies here. Don't exert time working on a project you can easily hire out for, and don't spend money trying to simply prove you're capable of handling it all when it would be best to pay for the expertise of a handyman or licensed contractor.

In light of all this, remember to be lenient with yourself in regards to craftsmanship (ability to do the work), time (ability to keep to a schedule; that is, finish all the work before your anticipated listing date), and cost (contractors can usually buy supplies at a discounted rate).

Improvements that Offer the Largest Payout

It's frequently thought that kitchens and bathrooms are areas of the home that offer the greatest return on renovation investment. While this can often be true, it isn't always the case and should never be considered a flat-out rule.

Focusing strictly on kitchens and bathrooms when

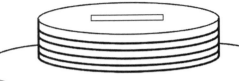

TIPS

Know the Difference: Handyman vs Contractor

Both can work on a wide variety of home projects, so what's the difference between the handyman and contractor? Basically: licensing.

Certain home repair or renovation jobs -- like electrical wiring, HVAC, plumbing, or building a home addition -- require a licensed contractor complete them. Other work -- like painting or small home repairs -- can be performed by a handyman.

Typically, real estate agents know who you should call for what kind of work (and will possibly be able to refer you to a trusted party). However, if they don't, they'll certainly be able to point you in the direction of someone who does.

considering which areas of your home to renovate to get the best return on investment (**ROI**) puts blinders to your property's true profit potential.

So before you go spending most of your budget on your kitchen and bath areas, consider exactly why and for whom you're doing the work. Once more, this falls back on knowing your target market and understanding what sort of buyer(s) would be interested in a property like yours.

Of course you'll be renovating to adapt to the needs of your target buyers, but there are obviously some features of your home that cannot be changed. Features like:

- property location;
- lot size, shape, and **zoning**;
- school district;
- community features;
- the house's architecture (e.g. Ranch, Colonial)

Consider these alternatives to the kitchen-bath renovations: improving curb appeal through new fencing or landscaping; installing new roofing or siding; basement remodeling; a deck, patio, or porch addition; or installing energy efficient windows throughout the home.

If you want to get creative, consider your buyer and the neighboring properties. Is it a rural area where homeowners tend to have outdoor storage? Consider adding a small shop or outbuilding to your property. Is it a family-centric neighborhood? Consider having a playground area put in the backyard for kids.

If you're at a loss, you can always talk to your real estate agent about what they think would be the most worthwhile projects for you to take on.

REMINDER...

Some building code problems hide in plain sight. Sellers unfamiliar with building code can easily miss things that could impede a quick sale.

For instance, many homes built in 1970 or earlier may not have GFCI outlets in necessary areas. Why not? Because GFCIs didn't become a requirement for certain rooms (e.g. bathrooms, garages, kitchens) until post-1971.

Similarly, the required space between stair balusters has become narrower in past years, so older homes with outdated railing may violate current code.

Remember to use the expertise of a licensed professional home inspector to your full advantage so you can pick out troublesome code violations -- and correct them -- *before* they create delays with your home's sale at an inopportune time.

When Upgrades Are Really Downgrades

First, understand this: Your home may be more personalized than you realize.

A home's style – rustic, contemporary, ultra-modern, or even something as specific as French Countryside – is so often less about the actual architecture of a building and more about how the living spaces (including the outdoor spaces) look and function.

For instance, a house may be styled as French Countryside externally (that is, a pale brick or stone exterior with wood and other natural accents), but that style doesn't necessarily transfer to the interior. The living spaces may be the complete opposite, perhaps outfitted with high-tech upgrades (e.g. USB outlets and smart thermostats) and a clean, sharp, black-and-white ultra-modern feel.

Using this example alone, we can see how styles and tastes can change the appeal of a house. One person might assume that everyone would want their home modernized with tech, even if the house looked rustic on the outside. Another person might wonder why anyone would buy a country-styled home and then "ruin" that vibe by "upgrading" the inside to be urbanely modern.

I make this point to show that what you might consider an upgrade – or even an "essential" – to a home really... isn't. Similar to the adage "One man's junk is another man's treasure," one man's improvement can also be another man's headache.

I've chosen a few common "upgrades" homeowners assume have good ROI, items that are commonly misjudged as being across-the-board improvements. While this isn't an exhaustive list, it's a good sampling of the kinds of projects you may want to avoid dedicating your time and money to:

- Pools, spas, or outdoor water features;
- Showy landscaping, especially involving plants that require a lot of care (e.g. hedges, rose bushes, topiary);
- Room-centric focus (e.g. modernizing one feature room while others are left outdated);
- Hidden features, like heated tile floors;
- Window treatments (e.g. wood slat shutters, curtains);

- Ultra-modern or tech-savvy extras (e.g. no-slam cabinet hardware, touch-free faucets, smart appliances);
- Features that put your home so far outside the norm for the neighborhood that it becomes awkward or showy (e.g. a driveway security gate in a largely gate-free community).

For more specifics on maximizing your ROI, talk with your agent about what home features lead to greater buyer interest in your area, or hire a home design consultant to guide you in the right direction.

The Importance of Staging

Staging is an important part of selling a property and is simply the act of visually preparing a private residence for sale. It's so important that a multi-BILLION dollar industry has been built around this key selling element! And, according to the National Association of Realtors®, 62% of sellers' agents believe staging decreases the amount of time a home is on the market.

Most people think staging is only for vacant homes, but that's simply not true. Even if the property you're selling is occupied, there are things you can do to improve your chances of attracting a buyer who'll pay your asking price.

If you have the budget for it, you can directly hire a home decorator or staging consultant to take care of [re] arranging the current furnishings or furnishing your house from scratch in preparation for showing. (Staging companies usually keep an inventory of items – like furniture, art, and general home décor – they use for their

Staging Your Home for Sale

What	Why	How
Depersonalize.	Your home is currently decorated with *you* in mind. But you're not selling to YOU; you're selling to someone else, and they can't envision themselves living there if photos of strangers are staring back at them from every wall, nor can they focus on what the house looks like if they're wondering if they know the people in the hallway photos.	• Reduce the number of family photos in living areas to just a few; let the space seem lived in and livable, but not occupied and unavailable; • Keep artwork generic; • Make the home feel unified by implementing finishing touches like solid, matching towels and removing items that feature unique designs and patterns.
Declutter.	Less is more. Too much stuff can make even large spaces feel small (or dirty).	• Clear off countertops, mantles, and walls of excess. • Maintain tidy bookcases and

		shelves.
		• Dust! (Don't forget ceilings and high corners.)
Tote toiletries away.	Toiletries left visible in bathrooms and showers give the feel of clutter, but occupants still need to use them.	• Think "hotel bathroom": Put toiletries on a decorative plate or in a tote that you can quickly store out of sight during showings.
Light it up.	Well-lit rooms – especially ones lit with natural light – give the impression of being cleaner, larger, and more inviting.	• Open drapes to allow as much natural light in as possible. • If windows are scarce, opt for one or two well-placed lamps per room.
Coordinate.	Again, think "hotel decor." Mismatched towels, furniture, etc. gives a confused, messy vibe.	• Put away mismatched towels and invest in matching sets. • The same goes for rugs, drapes, bedding, and throw pillows.

Table 3: Staging Your Home for Sale

jobs if homes they're working on are vacant.)

If hiring out for this task isn't part of your budget, don't worry. Staging doesn't have to be a daunting task. Just adhere to the guidelines in the table that begins on the next page and you'll be good to go.

Should I List During or After Construction?

Now that you know what you want to fix and how you'll do it, it's time to ask yourself if you should list during or after construction.

You may be thinking that listing after you're done with renovations is the only choice. After all, who wouldn't want a pristine home to show? Well, while "after" is correct, reality doesn't always cooperate.

If a wrench is thrown into your construction plans and delays progress, the selling season isn't going to wait for you to catch up. You're left with four options:

1. Keep the date and list your house on schedule, despite unfinished projects;
2. Move the listing date forward;
3. Forego the calendar and list whenever all construction is complete;
4. Or, if you're absolutely dedicated to listing in a certain selling season and with renovations complete (and if you're not in a hurry to sell), you can choose to list the following year.

Each of these options has its own pros and cons. Here's what you should know so you can decide wisely:

Option 1: Listing despite incompletion.

The downside of this choice is obvious: There's generally less appeal to buying a home with construction dust on the floor. Most people prefer to purchase a **turn-key property** and some won't even consider one that isn't. However, don't lose hope. There are ways lingering projects can work to your advantage.

First, showing a home with renovations in progress is obviously not ideal but it's also not a complete deal breaker, especially if the unfinished jobs are small. Consider this an opportunity to share your owner's pride with potential buyers; show them the quality of work you're putting into your home. This could bolster their confidence in you as a seller. They could feel more comfortable with the renovations you've already done knowing you've taken the time to do them right instead of throwing things together in a quick rush to sell, which is something other sellers may do that puts the quality, longevity, and value of recent fixes up for debate.

The last thing you want is a potential buyer walking into your unfinished home thinking, 'Gee, this house is a shambles. How can I know anything is done right? How can I know I won't have to fix all this stuff again later on?' To minimize or avoid those negative thoughts from popping up during showings, keep the in-progress projects as small as possible (that is, get big projects done *first!*) and to a minimum, with construction areas kept tidy. Don't let the projects become the elephant in the room; allow your real estate agent the freedom to talk with potential buyers about current construction, recently finished construction, and those things that may need to be worked on in the future by the new owner.

Remember: Buyers want transparency and honesty. They don't want to worry the home they're considering

STORY BOX

Staging

A very frustrated seller called saying her home had been listed with two other agents and had been on the market for over a year with no offers. Shocked, I asked what buyer feedback she'd received. She said they'd had very few showings and not much feedback to offer. I went to see her home for myself to determine the trouble.

Turns out the 1100 sq. ft. condo had too much furniture in it. The rooms were undefined; living spaces faded into one another. Buyers are very visual, and I suspected they couldn't envision themselves living in such jumbled spaces.

I hired a stager who rearranged furniture, balanced the rooms, and put unnecessary items in storage. Decluttering made the home feel larger and the spaces useable. After having photographs taken, we marketed the home heavily on social media.

It sold within 23 days for the price the seller wanted. She was a very happy lady!

purchasing is a lemon in disguise. So, the more they feel they can rely on you (and your home), the more likely they are to leave the showing with a positive vibe.

Option 2: Move the listing date.

While you're mid-renovation, things may come up that you don't expect. Even though you may have padded your timeline with extra days or months "just in case," that cushion may still not be enough. You're left with an incomplete home and a calendar that says you need to put it on the market *now*. What do you do?

Aside from ignoring the calendar and just forging ahead with renovations, you can choose to move your listing date forward beyond what you previously planned. Ideally the move won't be too far forward into the future and your timeline will allow you to at least catch the majority (or tail end) of the applicable selling season. You may still be able to get a good price for your property since you're not missing the season altogether, but you could miss out on some of the more eager buyers who shopped, and bought, early on.

Keep in mind that if your home pops up on the **MLS (Multiple Listing Service)** as a new listing among a plethora of older ones, that could be enough to grab the attention of buyers who started their shopping later in the game, or those buyers who have grown weary of all the same ol' houses that they've already seen (and didn't like) in the earlier part of the season.

Option 3: Forego the calendar.

If having your property move-in ready is more important to you than when you put it up for sale, you can opt to throw your selected list date out the window and just list whenever renovations are complete. This gives you time to complete projects without rush.

Obviously, the main problem with tossing the calendar is that you miss out on your selling season.

Another problem is less about the house and more about the owner's motivation. Without a goal date to provide incentive sometimes a lax attitude sets in, allowing projects to drag out longer than they should and thereby delaying the listing of the home even further, even if unintentionally.

If you're the kind of person who needs a deadline to keep you on your toes, I suggest setting a new listing date. Even if it's superfluous, at least you'll have something to aim for and keep you from dawdling about.

BUYER'S TIP...

Home Repairs? Trust Your Gut!

Although it would be great if sellers were completely honest about their home's maintenance history, we know that not everyone is quite so forthright.

Be aware of quality concerns, especially for a home's more recent projects. You know: Those ones a seller may have rushed through in order to list their home in time for the selling season.

Don't be afraid to ask who did the work, how it was done, or other specifics. In the end, trust your gut: if it feels like the work is iffy, you're probably right.

Option 4: Try again next year.

There's more flexibility in your options if you're in no hurry to sell. If showing a fixed up, turn-key property during your predetermined selling season tops your list of priorities, you can always just delay listing your house until the following year when you can catch the season at its start with your projects complete.

Doing this will give you plenty of opportunity to finish incomplete renovations carefully and correctly. If you left a few extra things off your to-do list in order to make goal, now you'll have time to do those.

The downside of this strategy is that there's no telling what the real estate market will look like next year. You could lose out if prices drop, the market slows, or mortgage interest rates go up.

The Takeaway

At the end of the day, this is what you need to know before you list your home:

- Research and select your selling season by knowing your target market;
- Decide how to handle your pre-listing inspection;
- Make a list of items you want to fix or renovate;
- Decide who will handle those tasks (DIY, handyman, or professional contractor);
- Stage your home; and
- If you run into a time crunch, decide how you'll proceed with your listing.

##

Notes

Chapter 4

Working with an Agent.

Do You Want an Agent? (99% Of the Time the Answer Is "Yes!")

Fixing something yourself as its benefits, one of which is full control over process, schedule, and outcome, in addition to the personal satisfaction many people get from the challenge and accomplishment of completing a home improvement project, even a small one.

However, DIY isn't always what it's cracked up to be. Behind the scenes of those home renovation shows—where the crews are all smiles while knocking down walls and hanging pretty new sconces—are the less glamourous aspects of the work: inspections, code enforcement, filing for permits, and troubleshooting the unexpected.

Hiring out has its own drawbacks. For one, if you're employed outside the home, you can't always be around to monitor or manage a handyman or construction crew when they're doing work on your house. Scheduling contractors on weekends when you're around can be difficult, too, since that's when everyone else wants them to do work and the contractors' schedules are tight or completely filled.

As with home improvement projects, there are positives and negatives to the actual selling of your property when debating between DIY (**For Sale by Owner**, aka **FSBO**) and hiring out (enlisting the help of a real estate agent). Of these two options, I'd strongly advise going with the latter 99% of the time.

So why don't I suggest selling without an agent? There are many smaller reasons that can be listed, but the vast majority of them fall into one or more of the following

categories:
- Reduced resources;
- Limited market knowledge;
- Lack of experience; and
- Biased interference.

I'll go over these four points in the next section in greater detail so that you can see what kind of value partnering with a real estate agent can be when it comes to selling your home.

FSBO: Not All It's Cracked Up to Be

If you're ready to list your home for sale and are leaning toward going the DIY route, take a moment to consider that you may be doing yourself a disservice by selling on your own.

Let's go one-by-one through those four categories listed in the previous section so you can see why having a real estate agent by your side is so valuable.

Reduced Resources

Putting a home up for sale and closing a sale on a home requires tapping into a lot of resources. Much happens behind the scenes of every listing that most people don't know about. When you sell on your own, the resources an agent would otherwise apply to the sale are all but absent. Those real estate agents' resources include:
- Time. If you have other life needs to handle, like work, school, and/or family obligations, you simply won't have as much time to dedicate to your listing as a real estate agent would.
- Connections. Agents have developed relationships

with people in the housing, real estate, and other related industries that can be useful in your efforts.

- Tools. Real estate agents have access to sales and marketing tools specific to real estate. Examples: MLS databases; up-to-date market-specific news; Realtor®-only forums and subscriptions; and information on how many days a property has been on the market or past history of sales.

Limited Market Knowledge

Unless you're a real estate agent, you're not working in, around, or with real estate on a daily basis. Because real estate is a fluid market—changing constantly throughout the year and, sometimes, on a daily basis—keeping abreast of pricing trends and other factors is critical to getting the best price on property.

As FSBO, you have both limited knowledge of the market as well as limited access to trends and important information that might be helpful in selling your property for the best price possible.

Lack of Experience

Like limited market knowledge, a lack of experience in everything from marketing and advertising to setting an initial price and negotiating the purchase can have a big impact on both the smoothness of the sales transaction and your net takeaway after closing.

Limited or lack of experience in selling property may also land you in legal hot water either now or in the future. You could inadvertently show bias to certain types of buyers (recall the **Fair Housing Act of 1968**).

Biased Interference

You like your home (or, at least, you once did). Even if your relationship with it may have dwindled and situations have changed which have led you to sell it, that doesn't mean you don't retain some pride in your property. After all, you've taken care of it, invested time and money into it, and, if you did any fixes or renovations before listing, it's even better now than it was before you decided to sell!

As a result, you have a bias when it comes to talking about your property. If you list on your own, you'll be the one talking to any potential buyers and showing them around the property and that bias, whether intentional or not, will come into play. And while it may seem that being over-enthusiastic about your property would be a good thing, it really isn't. Buyers not only like honesty and transparency, but also objectivity. You may be open and honest about the property when talking about it but that doesn't mean you're being objective. During a showing you may talk up quirks that don't bother you—or those you have simply grown accustomed to—but that a buyer might find intolerable. (Example: "The furnace is a little loud, but it creates a nice white noise to sleep to!") In such cases, your bias causes you to make an exception to a condition you'd otherwise consider problematic if it were in someone else's home or, even more, if it existed in a property you were looking to purchase.

If you find you're using adjectives like 'quirky,' 'unique,' or 'cute,' or uttering catchphrases like "gives it character" to describe your house, you may have a case of homeowners' bias on your hands! And, if that's the case, it's time to hire a real estate agent to represent you.

A real estate agent will act as a neutral party who can conduct showings and talk to potential buyers without tragically up- or down-selling your property. Sure, the right agent will have your best interests in mind, will highlight your home's best features and be honest about any less-than-ideal aspects, but they'll offer these insights in a way that has proven good and fair for their business, which, in the end, means it'll be good for yours.

(In case you're curious: When is that 1% of the time someone should go with the FSBO option? The answer: When you have a buyer lined up before you even think about listing your home. In a case like that, an agent's knowledge in listing and showing the home, as well as

REMINDER ...

Beware Ownership Bias

Bias about your property can be both positive and negative. It's easy to be excessively positive about your home if you're still in love with it.

However, if you've grown to hate your property and are just ready to wash your hands of it. You have ownership bias in this case, too!

You could inadvertently say something in the negative during a showing to a potential buyer that would change their opinion from "Maybe" to "Nevermind!"

Keep those opinions to yourself and trust your real estate agent to say the right thing at the right time to show your property in its best light to the attending home shopper.

in marketing the home, are no longer needed; you don't need to show the home, and an agent's sales experience doesn't make much difference when you have a buyer who is already standing by.)

Interviewing Agents

When enlisting the help of an agent with the sale of your property it's in your best interest to not only partner with an agent, but to partner with the right agent.

Like in other professions, not all real estate agents are created equal. For one, many if not most have preferences for the type of property they like to list. For example, some prefer to handle rural listings while others might lean toward single-family neighborhood homes while yet others specialize in high-end properties. Past training and sales experience; personal preference and tastes in homes; and general knowledge base all play a part in the preferences agents maintain.

You need to have a real estate agent on your team you can connect with. Their personality, in the form of communication skills, comes into play here. That's a tougher thing to interview for than just reviewing a resume, but feeling comfortable with your real estate agent on a personal level will make a huge difference in making the listing and sale of your home a smooth experience.

It's important to find the right agent to represent you. Remember: It's not only about experience. Many sellers automatically want to list with a real estate agent who's been in business for decades over the new (or new-ish) agent. Unfortunately, that's not always the best choice and could result in a lower priced sale, a longer listing, or an overall unfavorable experience for you, the buyer, or all parties involved.

Real estate agents are legal representatives. Would you go to court represented by a lawyer who you didn't connect with, who didn't care about you as a person or who didn't care about your greater well-being? Of course not! If you had your choice of lawyers, I doubt you'd simply hire the one who had the longest track record. The same goes for almost any other professional you might hire: doctors, mechanics, contractors, even pastors or counselors! These people, when hired, are intimately involved in your life's big decisions, so it's important that they don't only think of you as a means to an end.

Last but not least, it's important you not only have a licensed agent but one who calls themselves a **Realtor**®. Realtors® are kept to a strict code of ethics when it comes to conducting business as a real estate agent. Working with a Realtor® will ensure you are partnered with a trained and trustworthy professional who is dedicated to keeping their market knowledge up-to-date so they can provide their clients the best experience possible.

When meeting with a real estate agent to discuss listing your home with them, ask yourself questions like:

- Am I comfortable talking with this person on a professional level? On a personal level?
- Do I feel like this agent is intuitive about my needs?
- Do they ask the right questions? (Or, do they ask questions that I hadn't considered?)
- Are they supportive of my choices for listing/ schedule/price/et cetera, or do they constantly question or downplay my requests?
- Do I feel they genuinely care about me and my

property, or are they just looking to rack up listings (i.e. concerned about quantity over quality)?

If you're happy with the answers you get, good for you! You've likely found a great partner you'll work well with, an agent who will best represent you and your property from listing through to closing.

Getting on the Same Page

Once you've hired the agent you'll be working with, make sure you both have the same expectations.

Schedule a time to sit with your agent and go down the list of what you want to happen with your listing. Discuss everything from your asking price, to your **30-60-90-day price change schedule**, to what work you've done to the property, to what aspects of the property you realize are not up to par. If you want you can even hand them a list of items that you noted during your walk-through and discuss whether you want that list made available to interested buyers or not.

At this point, everything should be on the table. Open lines of communication are key to maximizing your sale. If you did your agent interviewing correctly, you'll feel comfortable enough with them to discuss whatever is necessary to attract a buyer as soon as possible.

During discussions with your agent you may find that some of your expectations for selling your home may be unrealistic. That's okay! The hope is that, as a result of finding an agent you're comfortable with, they'll offer more realistic goals and advise alternative solutions.

You and your real estate agent are a team, so keep lines of communication open and clear. If you can, put critical points—e.g. prices, dates—in writing so that nothing gets clouded in verbal transit. In addition to this, make sure you let them know what your communication preference is—texting, a phone call, email, etc.—so that they'll be able to contact you in the most efficient way possible and the chances of anyone getting frustrated with missed calls or messages is at a minimum.

Ultimately, being on the same page as your agent will help prevent any embarrassing or stressful mix-ups that eat up time and energy.

Taking Your Agent's Advice

As mentioned, you and your agent make up your primary home selling team. If you've followed the advice of the previous section, you have already combed through your expectations for the sale, from listing date and price to making clear at what intervals (or specific dates) you want the price to be reduced to when you'd like to conduct open houses (if at all).

Likewise, I expect your agent will offer their own expectations and suggestions for bettering your chances of selling your property faster and for more money. Don't take their experience for granted. Listen to their advice and consider all options, including ones you haven't thought of *and* ones that counter what you have in mind.

However, while they have your best interests in mind, at the end of the day this is *your* home for sale, not theirs. Even though you've hired your agent for their experience and market knowledge, don't feel obligated to agree to everything they say or suggest. Aside from the paperwork involving the listing and sale itself, much of what they tell you is *advice*, not law. How a real estate agent goes about

STORY BOX

30-60-90-Day Price Strategy

When one of my client sellers were being relocated to another state for work, they wanted to be out of their old home and into their new one before the new school term started. That only gave us three months to close!

We decided to set up an aggressive 30-60-90-day pricing and marketing strategy in advance of the listing: If we didn't get an offer in 30 days we would reset the price at 30-day intervals, up to two more times, until the property sold.

The strategy worked: We only had to change the price once. The home sold in its second month!

The family was able to move into their new home – the kids were off to the new school and the parents to the new job – within the desired time frame.

selling property lands strongly in the form of opinion and preference. If you were selective about choosing an agent to represent you, their sales methods should align pretty closely with how you envision your listing to be handled.

In short: Don't take your agent's opinion as law. If you're uncomfortable or unsure about a suggestion from your agent, simply ask: "Is that required to sell my property?" Take reasonable advice that lines up with your expectations and comfort levels, and leave that which doesn't.

Open Houses: Pros, Cons, & What to Do

Noting the example in the previous section about the real estate agent who put a lot of weight in open houses, it's about time to discuss what the pros and cons are of this popular selling tactic.

In real estate, an **open house** is a scheduled event wherein a listed property is made available for viewing by prospective buyers without them having to make an appointment. Having open houses was key to home sales prior to the widespread use of the Internet. Consider that today when buyers peruse listings online they are presented with multiple photos of the properties. Prior to the Internet, there was little other way for people to see the inside of homes up for sale unless they received flyers or brochures, or went to see the house in person. Therein lay the draw of the open house.

Some people believe that open houses are gimmicks for unseasoned agents to ease their way into the profession or are just advertising campaigns for real estate agents to sign new clients. While these are two reasons open houses are held, they hardly give the full story!

Open houses are less popular today than they used to be, no doubt. However, the practice still offers benefits to not only real estate agents but also to sellers and remains a sales method worth considering.

Pros

What people take away from seeing something in person is completely different than what they get from viewing photographs of the same thing on the Internet.

The same principle applies to an open house: If executed properly, an open house is first an *experience* for the visitor, a sales method second. It should leave a memorable impression that will positively influence the visitor's tendency to make contact with the seller and/or seller's agent. An online-only listing, on the other hand, leaves little impression and risks easily fading from memory as just one of many listings seen on a computer screen.

Prospective buyers will be able to better appreciate the home's upgrades, renovations, and finer features that might be missed in photographs or in a quick peek with an agent in the lead. This can lead to a sense of increased value and perhaps an offer on the table.

An open house is also a great way to start talking to potential buyers about what they're looking for. Positive conversations build a buyer's trust (recall the importance of honesty and transparency) and provide opportunity to discuss ways you might come to a sales agreement.

For instance, let's say a buyer views a home and they're mildly interested minus one thing: they hate the bathroom tiles. They don't have any interest in getting into a project (they're looking for a turn-key property) and the likelihood is slim of them approaching the seller's real estate agent to ask if the seller will change the tiles for them. If no conversation is had, the buyer walks out and both the seller and the seller's agent are none the wiser.

Wouldn't you want to know if the sale of your home depended on whether or not you updated some tiles?

By having conversation with open house visitors your real estate agent could discover not only what people are seeing that they *don't like*, but also could happen upon an opportunity where a buyer will gladly put in an offer if only just one more thing in the home were changed.

Cons

Despite their benefits, open houses have declined in popularity. As mentioned, it is believed there's little reason to physically show a property if photographs can be made available online for potential buyers to see. People are able to view dozens of homes online in the time it would take to drive to and from your open house event. While the experience of the open house may be worthwhile, many home shoppers are more drawn to the power of quantity over quality. That is, they find more value in viewing more listings than in experiencing a home in person.

Open houses are not only time consuming for the shopper but also for the seller and/or seller's agent. The ROI of time put into advertising, arranging, and conducting an open house is questionable. Many real estate agents don't find the return worth the cost.

Nosey neighbors may see open houses as a legitimate excuse to come into your home and snoop around. Not only is this annoying (especially if you are not on good terms with your neighbor), but it takes away from the quality experience you're trying to offer to serious buyers.

For example, the hosting agent won't immediately know the difference between a nosey neighbor and a legitimate buyer, and may spend valuable time and energy talking to an uninterested party while a legitimate buyer walks in and walks out, ignored and feeling put off by a lack of personal attention from the representing agent. Did a sale just walk in and then *out* your front door? Sadly, you'll never know!

Speaking of sales walking out, it's unclear whether or not open houses actually result in the sale of the featured property. Such statistics are hard to determine and much of the notion of open houses' viability is based solely on independent real estate agents' experiences, which vary greatly from one agent to another. As mentioned before, many real estate agents take advantage of hosting open houses to improve their networks and to meet potential new clients, things that don't directly benefit owners of the home they're showing.

Finally, open houses bring up security concerns. After all, you are inviting absolute strangers into your home to take a look around! Open houses are opportunities for criminals and potential thieves to scope for goods without being suspected of anything malicious. This presents a property liability and possible personal danger, especially if the home is currently being lived in.

What to Do

If you've decided that holding one or more open houses is right for you and your property, there are some things you can do to maximize the selling power of your event. These things are outlined in the table following this section.

If you've hired a real estate agent, they'll likely have all these things in mind and taken care of for you. Still, it's good to be in the know so you understand what your agent is doing and why they may ask certain things of you.

##

Holding An Open House

Before the showing...

Keep it clean.	A clean home obviously shows better than a messy one. If you've followed the protocol for cleaning and decluttering from Chapter 3 (Table 3), then you're already there. Check this one off your list!
Stage, Stage, STAGE!	You need to decorate the house neutrally enough so that any visitor can envision themselves living there. Your real estate agent will typically handle this detail (Chapter 3, *Staging*).
Spread the word.	Advertise your open house with flyers, mailers, newspaper ads, or get creative by posting a video on social media. Your agent will generally take care of ads in common market outlets, both in print and online, in addition to placing street signage. However, that doesn't mean you can't help by sharing via your personal social media pages. Spread the word wherever you can, focusing on areas your

	target market lives.
Spread the word. - cont'd	
Signage: Use it!	Signs aren't only good for Open House Day, but also make for good buzz. People on the look-out for a home can do a drive-by beforehand if they see signs pointing the way. (This is some-thing your agent should take care of in addition to handling flyers and online advertising.)
Invite other agents.	Real estate agents talk to other agents in their networks about their listings and clients; it's how they're able to increase their chances of making deals, fast. As part of advertising, postcards or letters should be sent to area real estate offices or agents to invite them to the open house. They're the ones with clients looking for homes, after all, and one real estate agent could mean a handful or more potential buyers in your pocket.
Scope out the competition.	Visit other open houses in the area to get an in-person experi-ence of what it should feel like as an attendee. If you go to a few put on by different real

Scope out the competition. - continued	estate agents, you may even begin to notice what works and what doesn't, not to mention see what other properties like yours have to offer.

The day of...

Open House on Listing Day	You can opt to do more open houses later but holding an open house on the day the property is listed will give serious buyers a chance to see the goods immediately. You'll still have to advertise ahead of time, of course, but this just builds interest and anticipation, making people feel like your home is something worth looking forward to!
Smells make a difference.	I'm not only talking about neutralizing those smells you've gone **nose blind** to, but also adding scents that are pleasing. Baking a tray of cookies is a simple and popular way to improve the open house experience through smell and also provides visitors a snack while they peruse the property.

Smells make a difference. - continued	You can opt to put in air fresheners throughout the house, though know that many people experience adverse reactions (e.g. headache, nausea) to the chemicals contained in air fresheners, so you may accidentally be coaxing buyers away by using artificial scents.
Offer more information.	Offer visitors an attractively designed handout that gives additional information about the home, including area schools, amenities, and features that can't be seen by the naked eye (e.g. a whole house humidifier that's tucked away in the basement or a floor heating system hidden beneath the hardwood).
Get names.	Your agent should encourage visitors to sign in. This way they can collect names, phone numbers, and/or emails so they can follow up with visitors about their experience and answer any questions they may have. This creates a direct and open line of communication for that honesty buyers seek.

Seller's Secrets

Promote a Good *Walk Score*® Rating

Walkability can be a huge draw for home shoppers these days. Not only does it help people feel a deeper connection with their neighborhood and encourage better health, but walkability is attractive to families who walk together as a way to bond.

And, according to a 2017 National Association of REALTORS® poll, 6 in 10 home shoppers said they'd pay a little bit more for a home in a walkable community!

If your property has a high Walk Score® rating, promote it!* You'll attract the attention of buyers who are willing to pay extra for that unique and healthy benefit.

Walk Score® is a private company that provides a very popular walkability index for properties in the US, Canada, and Australia. Visit WalkScore.com to find your property's walkability rating.

Get names. - continued

BONUS: If your agent doesn't already, suggest they make a short note about each visitor learned through conversation (ex. children, pets, special interests, etc.). Building repertoire by showing interest in them as a person can go a long way.

Get names. - continued	In short: Your real estate agent should make the open house a memorable experience, not just one of a dozen open houses the buyer has attended.
Engage!	Your real estate agent should put away distractions and engage with visitors, starting with a warm greeting. This allows buyers the chance to put their guards down, ask questions, and start a conversation about what they're looking for. This approach also gives your agent the opportunity to up-sell and forge connections that could prove memorable enough to put your house ahead of the competition Visitors should be free to explore yet feel they can approach the agent easily with questions or for conversation. (This is more a reminder for your agent, since you, the homeowner, should not be attending your own open house.)
Follow up...	
Call back.	After a few days, your agent should contact the open house guests using the contact information they provided on the sign-in sheet. The

Call back. - continued	purpose of the follow up is to remind buyers that the home remains available; it is not to hard sell the property, as hard sales tactics generally turn buyers off.

Table 4: Holding an Open House

Notes

Chapter 5

Let's Talk Money.

People have different primary goals for selling property. For some, it's to relocate themselves and their families. For others, it could purely be a profiteering venture. Whatever the primary reason, all sellers have this in common: They want to come out financially on top.

Selling a home involves spending money in order to make money. You spend money on renovations and fixes (including construction and building permits for larger jobs); on inspections; on commission to your agent; and perhaps even the prep work for an open house (e.g. staging, food), if your real estate agent doesn't consider this a **cost of doing business** and absorb the expense themselves. All in all, costs can add up quickly!

But don't let those costs deter you. By thoroughly researching the market and allowing your agent to be your guide throughout the sales process, you can rest assured you'll be on the plus side when closing time comes.

In this chapter, we'll go over the basics of the costs of selling, how appraisals work and how a home's value is determined, as well as options like carrying the buyer's loan or offering incentives.

Get Appraised

Before anything happens, you may want your home's value to be determined by a qualified **appraiser**, a professional trained in seeking out and identifying all aspects of a property to determine your property's current market value. This value gets used in multiple ways: Not only will you and your agent use your home's appraised value to set a listing price, but interested buyers may ask to see the **appraisal** report (and/or the **comparative market analysis report (CMA)**, which is compiled by the listing agent) prior to making an offer so that they can determine for themselves if the listed price is fair.

Additionally, the loan officer or mortgage lender involved in the sale may want an appraisal report to assure the sale numbers align in the best interests of the bank. (Keep in mind the lender may not care about your appraisal and opt to do their own. Again, much depends on your location and the lender the buyer is using.)

I believe a CMA is more important than an appraisal for a number of reasons. Though both appraisals and CMAs include the data from currently listed and recently sold homes in your neighborhood that are most like your home in appearance, features, and general price range, an appraiser has no vested interest in promoting your property. Your agent will use your property's highlights to show its greatest value, giving you the best opportunity for making the most profit.

In order for you to receive the highest price for your property, you need to get the highest value on your CMA report. That's why it's important for you to understand what data real estate agents use to write up a CMA and what items you can influence to benefit you the most.

How Value is Determined

When collecting data for a CMA, a real estate agent will take both an interior *and* exterior assessment of a home. They'll consider factors such as comparable property sales in the area (**comps**), square footage, condition, age, layout, upgrades, and others. They'll do a fairly thorough home inspection (though it won't be as complete as a home inspector's analysis), from checking light switches and visual problems, to making note of any obvious exterior foundation or drainage issues, to going up on the roof to check the condition of shingles and gutters. During all this, the agent should be taking *lots* of photos to document and support their findings.

Behind the scenes, your real estate agent will check with external sources—courthouse records, data vendors, and the MLS, to list a few—to assure their report is complete and everything is disclosed that needs to be.

While a real estate agent won't be doing as complete a job as a real home inspector, you'll get a really good idea from their CMA of what will be noticed by buyers who come to take a look around. Using this information, you can decide whether or not you want to do any work on the house (in addition to any fixes or renovations you've already completed), or just sell it as-is.

Hopefully, though, your agent will tell you these things upfront so you're not left guessing or they're not left having to redo a CMA because the initial report was less than glowing.

Understanding Price Differences: CMA vs Listing vs Sale

While a CMA is a very handy tool in the selling process, the value put on your home is not a hard and fast number that you need to comply to within your listing.

Sellers sometimes feel that the reported value is too low—that there is additional value or other features of the home that aren't considered in the report—and list the property higher than the suggested price. The listing price can go the opposite way, too, where sellers decide it's too high and decide to list below the reported value.

Also, just because buyers are presented with a CMA prior to making an offer doesn't mean they have to agree with the number. Consider again that not all perks are perks to everyone, like the example used previously about the swimming pool. So even if your real estate agent counts a swimming pool as a plus in the value column, a buyer may consider a pool a minus and offer below the suggested CMA value.

You'll Need Money, Too!

Selling a home can be as much an investment as it is a profitable endeavor. In the beginning you'll need cash in

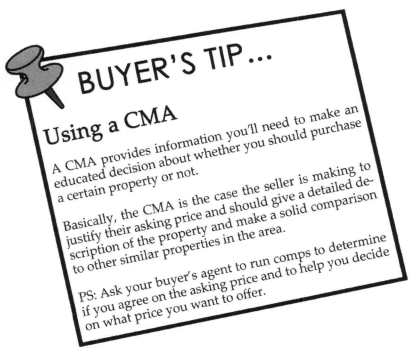

BUYER'S TIP...

Using a CMA

A CMA provides information you'll need to make an educated decision about whether you should purchase a certain property or not.

Basically, the CMA is the case the seller is making to justify their asking price and should give a detailed description of the property and make a solid comparison to other similar properties in the area.

PS: Ask your buyer's agent to run comps to determine if you agree on the asking price and to help you decide on what price you want to offer.

order to do what has to be done to complete the sale.

Many of these costs were covered in previous chapters—to include money spent on fixes and renovations, inspections, marketing efforts, et cetera—but there are also others to consider that won't come into play until an offer has been made and the sale is well under way (or complete).

The largest of these costs is your agent's commission. The exact number will depend on the terms you agree to. For example, 5-7% commission is traditional in my area (Hershey, PA), with 5% commission offered for new construction and 6% for resale.

Other costs that can catch sellers by surprise include the following:

Loan Payoff & Associated Fees

If you still owe on your home, the remaining amount owed on your loan will be subtracted from the sales total. In addition, your lender may charge an early payoff fee when you sell the property. Whether you'll be charged this early payoff fee depends on the details of your specific loan, so it's a good idea to contact your mortgage lender to see if such a fee will come into play when you sell. It's no fun being surprised with a charge you didn't know you'd get!

In addition, any home equity line of credit attached to the house will also need to be paid off at time of the closing.

Transfer taxes and recording fees

These are fees and taxes you'll pay to your state or local government offices in exchange for them handling various recordkeeping aspects, such as the transfer of title from you to the buyer.

Title insurance fees

Title is a group of rights the owner has on their property. Upon sale of that property, those rights are transferred to the new owner(s). However, there are rare occasions when the transfer is incorrectly recorded, resulting in legal trouble down the road in the form of a **lien, encroachment** (or other **encumbrance**), legal claim, or defect. **Title insurance** protects owners and lenders against property loss or damage due to problems with the property's title.

Most mortgage lenders require title insurance be purchased by the buyer(s) prior to lending.

Closing Costs

Closing costs are expenses above and beyond the price of the property in a real estate transaction. Basically, they're the costs incurred to close a sale. They include all the previously listed expenses—loan payoff, transfer taxes, title insurance fees—and more, depending on what is negotiated with the buyer during the sale. It's fairly typical these days for a seller to offer to pay part or a portion of a buyer's closing costs, but that is by no means a requirement.

Offering to pay closing costs is a positive good faith effort on the seller's part, so I'd suggest taking it into consideration when calculating your final profit.

When the time comes, discuss in detail with your agent how you'd like to settle these costs.

Carrying the Loan: Pros and Cons

There could be a number of reasons why either party

doesn't want to involve a bank or mortgage lender in the transfer of property. In such cases, the seller may offer to carry the loan for the buyer. Carrying the loan means the seller becomes the bank that handles the finances involved in the sale, negotiating everything from **down payment** to interest rate to monthly payment schedule with the buyer(s).

In cases where the seller is willing to also serve as bank, listings are generally marked as **Owner Will Carry (OWC)** so that prospective buyers will know up front that this is a financing option for them. There are instances where buyers don't want to seek financing from a typical bank and will seek out OWC properties specifically.

If carrying the loan is a route you're open to taking, tell your agent up front so that they can include the OWC marker on the listing.

Other Incentives: Should You Offer Any?

Sometimes a buyer is on the fence on whether or not they should move forward with making an offer. Incentives can give these fence-sitting buyers that extra nudge toward making an offer and speed you toward closing.

Incentives certainly aren't required, but they can sweeten the deal. How much they sweeten it depends of course on what exactly you're offering and how valuable those incentives are to the buyer. Again, different things present different values to different people, so offering a washer/dryer may make a huge difference to a buyer who doesn't have those appliances, but will mean little to one who already owns a washer/dryer set. (Not many people aim to have two sets of laundry machines!)

Incentives can be material objects—like the washer/

dryer set used in the example above—or they can be monetary, like interest rate buy-downs or prepaid HOA fees. They can also include things like:

- Closing cost credits;
- Additional buyers' broker commission;
- Monetary allowance to cover future and foreseeable home repairs;
- Furniture and window treatments;
- Appliances;
- Pre-paid utilities; or
- Pre-paid homeowner services (e.g. landscaping, housekeeping, pool maintenance).

Truly, anything can qualify as an incentive. It all comes down to what the buyer finds appealing and what you're willing to negotiate. Again, your agent can discover what a buyer might find intriguing if the time is taken to understand the buyer's personal tastes and preferences. The buyer's agent can be of assistance in this matter—certainly they'd like to see a sale close, too!

As for timing, incentives can be made clear up front or you can keep them up your sleeve, so to speak, to use later on during negotiations at the table. How you utilize incentives is completely up to you, though your agent may have ideas on whether or not incentives should be included in the MLS listing details.

When Time Isn't Money

When selling your property, obviously the end goal is to come out in the black and as much in the black as possible. As you've read through this book, hopefully you've come to realize that time really is money, so the faster you can sell, the better.

However, like most rules, this one can be broken. There is a point at which rushing the sale to save time can actually *cost* you cash! Let's quickly examine how that can happen so you can avoid such a costly mistake.

Rushing the Sale

Unless you're on a strict schedule that requires you sell your home right away, being in too big a hurry and rushing a sale can cost you in the end. In an effort to close faster, you may offer incentives and extras that you otherwise wouldn't or that you never really had to in order to close the deal.

For example, maybe you didn't intend to throw in the washer/dryer as part of the deal, but a buyer insists those be included otherwise they walk. You could let them go and wait for another buyer. However, if you're either in a hurry or are worried another buyer won't come along anytime soon, you might just give in and give the appliances up. Sure, you sold your home, but now you have to buy a new washer-dryer set for yourself!

In an alternate scenario using the same incentive, a seller's eagerness could cause them to jump the gun and offer the washer/dryer before they even arrived at that point in the negotiations. The buyer would have made an offer without the appliances thrown in, but now they get free laundry machines too? Wonderful! Except now you, the seller, are out at least a few hundred dollars because you need to buy new laundry machines.

Take cues from your real estate agent on whether or not you should rush or wait. You may feel like you're sitting around twiddling your thumbs, waiting for things to happen, but that's all part of the process. Simply put, there is no instant gratification in real estate, and waiting is part of the game.

Legal Ramifications to Rushing

While you may begin to feel seller's anxiety (especially once an offer is on the table), don't give in to the notion that things aren't happening fast enough! Some sellers who fall prey to their impatience make the critical mistake of interfering with their agent's process by going around them and talking with the buyer (or the buyer's agent) directly. Not only does it do a disservice to the seller, but it's also rude and unprofessional! After all, you've hired your agent to do a job. Trust that they, their experience, and their process will be effective and get you to your goal as quickly and as efficiently as possible. Going around your agent to discuss or negotiate terms with the buyer or buyer's agent directly will cloud the water. Certain things will get communicated that shouldn't be (or the right things will get *mis*communicated) and at best the buyer will walk away, irritated, and, at worst, there could be legal claims of damages, loss, discrimination, false representation, or false advertising (i.e. nondisclosure of or falsified property conditions) brought against you, which could mean lawyers, court, and more money spent on your part. It's simply not worth it.

Leave the talking to your real estate agent so that things are accurately and properly communicated to all parties and you're kept out of legal hot water.

##

TIPS

Things You Can Do To Help Your Agent

While you shouldn't get involved directly with the buyer or buyer's agent to help move the sale along, there are ways you can assist in the listing and sale of your home.

Consider these options and discuss with your agent what other ideas they may have on how you can help improve the chances of you finding the right buyer, faster.

- Share your listing on social media.
- Keep your schedule flexible for showings and open houses.
- Return calls from your agent quickly to avoid any delays.

Notes

Chapter 6

Interviewing Buyers.

Did I Just Say "Interview"?

Yes, I did.

You've already gone through the process of interviewing a real estate agent (Chapter 4) and, now that marketing has begun and your home is listed and being shown, it's time to interview your buyers to see if they're serious about making a deal.

Nobody wants to waste their time with lookie-loos whose arms you have to twist (or shower with extras and incentives) in order to get to close on the sale.

Ideal buyers come prepared. They've done their homework on the current market and know what to expect; they've researched financing options and know their own finances—they know what kind of payment they can afford, what their loan options are, have a **pre-qualification** or **pre-approval** letter in-hand, have a down payment ready to go, et cetera—and, last but not least, they know exactly what they want in a home. These types of buyers have possibly been looking for a while but haven't found "the one" yet. With any luck, your property could be it!

This isn't to say that those new to the market won't close on a sale or aren't serious about buying. Many are. However, new shoppers may not have gotten around to getting their ducks in a row (for instance, they don't have their finances in order or a pre-approval/qualification letter ready) and getting those things arranged could take some time.

Generally speaking, your real estate agent should be able to let you know if you should be holding your breath or not about a particular buyer. Real estate agents, especially those who have worked in the industry a while, have honed their skills and can intuitively tell whether or not a buyer is worth pursuing and should be following up with or told the incentives you're willing to offer. (For some buyers, meeting the homeowner in person and making a one-on-one connection is just enough to give them confidence in the property. However, discuss this with your agent first. Per the previous chapter, you don't want to get in your own way—or in your agent's way—when it comes to closing the sale!)

Keep in mind that *your* intuition is also a valuable tool and shouldn't be ignored! If you get the feeling a buyer isn't really serious, tell your agent so. Make it clear to them that you don't want to waste your time with questionable buyers. Remember: Your pre-established window for selling is short and the selling season won't last forever. Recall that 30-60-90-day price change schedule you and your real estate agent set down? That's still in play, and you don't want to waste any of your precious time dawdling with someone who isn't serious.

Speaking of which: What *are* the signs a buyer isn't serious? Here are a few:

- They're shady about or outright dodge questions about financing or how long they've been in the market for a home;
- They reschedule appointments for showings one or more times;
- They're hasty with the showing and don't spend much time actually looking at property;

- They make excuses for delays in the purchasing process;
- They don't have any letters prepared from a lender;
- They're nitpicky about the property and point out all its faults; and
- They off-handedly hint — or aggressively demand — at wanting extras and incentives before (or even after!) they've put an offer on the table.

There are other ways to tell if a buyer isn't serious, but these are the most obvious ones. Buyers who show these signs of false interest or blunt disinterest aren't worth entertaining. You and your agent had better spend your time elsewhere.

Finding a Buyer

Before you or your agent can interview potential buyers, you first have to find them.

Understanding a particular buyer's motives for shopping the market will help you pitch your home to them in the right way (for example, highlight the right features during a showing or use the right "hot words" in advertisements) to garner the most interest and, therefore, get the most money!

Finding buyers starts off by finding **leads**, prospective buyers who have been targeted through information sharing and/or collecting. That information is gathered through open houses (per the sign in sheet; Chapter 4); through relationships with other agents who have clients looking to buy; or by sending out feelers through **direct mail marketing**.

Another way to find leads is through the use of **social media marketing**. Social media marketing is the specific use of social media platforms to promote a product, in this case a home. Most social media platforms have built-in tools that can help your real estate agent zero in on people searching for homes in your area, as well as analyze the effectiveness and reach of the ad they are posting.

Types of Buyers: A Quick Review

Let's not spend too much time recapping this, but recall from Chapter 3 the section on determining your target buyers and how it may be helpful to understand who you're looking for so you can sell faster. In that chapter, we went over why selecting a type of target buyer is important. Here, I offer a list of a few types.[†] (Note that it is possible for a buyer to fall into more than one type category.)

Turn-key

A turn-key property is one that is completely finished and ready to move into. For most shoppers, the ideal situation involves a house exactly as they want it when they make the purchase. For the vast majority, though, this just isn't the case. Buyers usually go into a purchase knowing there will be some kinds of home projects in their future.

However, there are buyers who will avoid projects altogether without negotiation. These are buyers who are *specifically* on the lookout for a turn-key property; they

---

[†]   This is not an extensive list, but a starting point to begin discussion with your real estate agent about what type of buyer you're looking for and to whom the sales strategy should be aimed toward.

don't want to be confronted with projects or think about the property's "potential". For these types of buyers, the home is either ready or it isn't—there is no in between—and words and phrases like "potential," "could be," or "a little work" are deal breakers.

Fixer

On the other end of the spectrum is the buyer who is *actively seeking* a project home to tackle (otherwise called a **fixer-upper**). They like to see a property for its possibilities rather than its current condition; they enjoy the creative challenges of home improvement. These buyers don't mind if a property has blemishes since they're willing to look beyond those faults.

Note that within this category there are variations on what a buyer is and isn't willing to spend money on fixing; some are willing to spend a lot and do a lot (for example, are willing to take on in depth projects, like installing new electrical or plumbing), while others only seek to fix cosmetic issues (ex. new paint and flooring).

Fixers may be purchasing property for their personal use or they may be seeking to flip it for profit. Whatever the case may be, they don't want perfection.

As-Is

Consider the As-Is buyer as being halfway between the turn-key and fixer types. They're not specifically seeking a fixer-upper nor are they on the lookout for a home in perfect shape and order. Don't think, though, that because they're willing to take a property as-is that they don't know what they want or have expectations as to how a property should be. These types of buyers are probably going to do some hard negotiating on price because they consider the fact that they're accepting the property without additional demands as a bonus for the seller, which is true to a point: You won't have to pay up for additional improvements or incentives, but that ease comes at its own cost.

Flipper

A buyer who is **flipping** properties is one who is seeking to purchase at a below-market rate, invest in renovations, then resell. (Though flipping can be considered buying at a low or reasonable price and waiting for the market to improve to resell, that's not typically what is meant by the term. Generally, a home flipper is one who "flips" the house from bad to good condition to sell at a profit all under a quick turnaround.)

Flippers are usually looking for a bargain more than most because they will invest time and money into the property before relisting it. Flippers also aren't looking for a home in perfect condition; they're willing to invest **sweat equity** as well.

Remember that flippers won't be living in the house, so they don't care about and aren't looking for personal touches that speak to them directly. They're seeking generic qualities and perks that appeal to a broad base of home shoppers so they can resell. Because of this, trying to sell to their personal tastes simply won't work.

It's also valuable to note that a number of flippers are real estate agents themselves. This means they'll have inside and up-to-date information on the market and trends, which makes them more apt than a traditional buyer when it comes time to negotiate a deal.

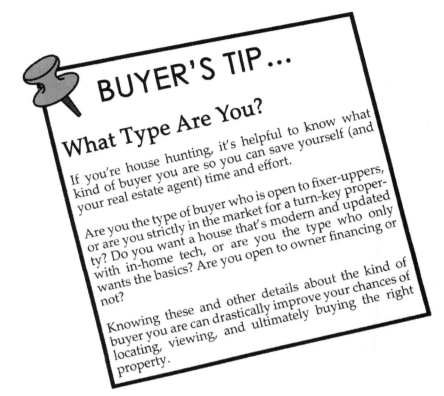

BUYER'S TIP...

What Type Are You?

If you're house hunting, it's helpful to know what kind of buyer you are so you can save yourself (and your real estate agent) time and effort.

Are you the type of buyer who is open to fixer-uppers, or are you strictly in the market for a turn-key property? Do you want a house that's modern and updated with in-home tech, or are you the type who only wants the basics? Are you open to owner financing or not?

Knowing these and other details about the kind of buyer you are can drastically improve your chances of locating, viewing, and ultimately buying the right property.

Between Listing & Offer: What You Can Do to Help

Most homeowners want to be helpful and be involved in the sale of their property. It's difficult to sit around and watch the days tick by, waiting for the phone to ring with the call that a buyer has been found. At the same time, nobody wants to impede the process by stepping on their agent's toes.

So, what's a seller to do?

There are ways you can assist in the selling process

without getting in the way, specifically through use of the Internet.

Social Media

Social media sites are an easy way you can help spread the word about your property without interfering with your real estate agent's strategy. They include sites like Facebook, Twitter, Instagram, and Reddit, to name a few of the more popular ones.

Consider these steps when posting your property on one or more of your social media pages:

1. Take a photo of a special feature of your property that isn't well known (and, ideally, one that isn't highlighted on your agent's advertisements), like a picturesque view or a photo of the community playground, and post it on one or more social media pages (Facebook, Twitter, Instagram, etc.).

2. Add a short snippet of information about what's in the photo.

3. Learn and use the **hashtags** that are prevalent for your area's real estate market – for example, #ruralrealestate or #newhomelisting – so that the postings are easily located and shared with the right crowd.

4. Include your agent's contact information or a link to their website in the photo's description.

5. Remember to direct any individuals asking questions through direct messaging to your real estate agent. Don't get involved aside from sharing the photos, lest you say something unhelpful, biased, or even illegal!

Posting to social media on a regular basis (think once per day or every other day) is a great way to offer your unique insight as the homeowner and give your real estate agent's marketing efforts a boost without getting in the way.

YouTube

Although few users see it as much more than a place to watch videos, technically YouTube is considered a social media site. However, because it's viewed so differently and used differently than other social media sites, it deserves a separate section on how to best use it to highlight your home for sale.

First, know that you don't have to narrate what's happening in the video! Narrations often come off as awkward or too scripted (aka fake sounding), which turns people off. Allow your video to speak for itself. If you don't like the idea of a soundless video, consider adding background music instead of a narration to fill the space.

If, however, you feel a narration would help to explain what the viewer is seeing, consider writing out a short script and reading it as you record the walkthrough. This will keep you from going off-topic, saying something you don't want to out of nervousness, or inundating your narration with awkward pauses and unattractive "Um's".

Second, use high quality video. A blurry, fuzzy image does little to inspire interest.

Third, make sure the area you're videoing is (1) well lit, and (2) void of personal effects (e.g. jewelry, firearms) that might tempt would-be thieves.

Finally, remember that people respond best to short video clips. Today's busy lifestyle prevents most people

Is This Buyer *Serious* or *Not?*
How to Tell.

SERIOUS	*NOT* SERIOUS
They're eager to let you and your realtor know they have pre-approved financing.	They answer vaguely to your or your realtor's questions.
They schedule and *show up* for a private viewing. They may even arrive early to the appointment!	They reschedule appointments one or more times, cancel without reason, or are no-shows.
They arrive on time (or early) then take their time during the showing to get a good look around.	They're hasty during the showing and don't spend much time actually looking at property.
They ask questions that *aren't* answered by the sales flyer.	They're nitpicky about the property and point out all its faults.
They have letters from a lender prepared to show your real estate agent.	They make excuses for delays in the purchasing process.
They're pleased with extras and incentives, but don't expect them.	They want extras and incentives before they've put an offer on the table.

Table 5: Is This Buyer Serious or Not? How to Tell.

from being able to sit down at length and watch long sales videos online, so avoid uploading videos longer than three minutes. Short videos (a) maintain viewers' attention, and (b) mean you can take *more* videos, and more videos means you can share them more often on your other social media pages.

Similar to your other social media posts, offer a short summary of what's in the video as part of the video's description and direct questions to your agent.

A final note on safety: *Never* publish the address of the property on social media! Interested parties can locate the home by contacting your real estate agent. If you publicize the address you're just giving potential criminals not only a quick look around the inside of your home (and the belongings stored there), but a floorplan of it as well.

##

S T O R Y   B O X

The Reverse Offer: Creative Selling

A homeowner who'd attended one of my seminars approached me asking for help selling his home, an all-brick ranch with nice extras. It needed some work, like fresh exterior trim paint, but nothing big.

Showings all resulted in the same negative feedback: The house was placed far back on the lot making the backyard too small. Buyers wanted space for their kids to play! One shopper seemed interested, but said they weren't ready to buy because their out-of-state home needed to sell first. A big yard wasn't crucial to them, so I knew this house was a great match. I quickly called the seller, suggesting that we make a **reverse contingent offer**.

By reaching out with a creative solution we were able to close on the hard-to-sell home soon after.

Notes

Chapter 7

Congratulations!
You Have an Offer!

I f all goes well, you'll have an offer in no time. Congratulations! But, as excited as you may be, remember that the sale isn't complete yet and there's still plenty to do. Each state is different when it comes to the details, but for the most part there are a few things that will happen—and that you need to do—before you see a check in your hand.

Consider the following bits of advice for when you get that phone call from your agent saying an offer has come in.

Step 1: Stay Calm.

It's natural to get excited when the offer (or multiple offers) comes in. You should be! At the same time, though, don't let your excitement get the better of you. Because the end is near in sight, it's easy to be excitable, but giving in to such feelings can cause sellers to do more harm to themselves than good.

Allowing emotions to take over can result in overeagerness, which can lead to mistakes like poor negotiating; improperly filling out or forgetting to fill out forms; failing to pay attention to the sales process and things you need to take care of; or missing critical deadlines.

Conversely, be aware of overcompensating for your excitement, too. Sellers may intentionally act aloof and excessively coolheaded in the midst of the hubbub, thinking their neutral front will prevent the buyer from thinking they have the upper hand. This can backfire, too: The buyer may feel you don't like their offer and withdraw it.

One thing that may help to curb any excessive enthusiasm is, once you read the offer, to set it aside. Come back to it in a little while after the initial feelings wear off so you can think more rationally and clearly.

(It's important to note, though, that there are generally time frame restrictions written into the real estate contract. Be attentive to these, as adhering to them can make or break the sale. An example is that you'll have a certain number of days to give an answer back to the buyer on whether you **accept** their offer or not. If you need more time to think than the restriction allows, consider asking for an extension. Your real estate agent can help you with this process.)

Overall, it's important to just stay calm when an offer comes in without acting indifferent. An offer is a wonderful thing—you have every right to be happy! Let that happiness thrive and rely on your agent for guidance in how to respond appropriately to the buyer's offer.

Step 2: Negotiations: Your Yeses and Nos.

When you're looking at the offer(s), of course the first thing to consider before anything else is what price the buyer is offering to pay.

You likely know what **net profit** you want to get out of your home's sale, so at this point you and your agent can do a little math to determine if the offer minus any expenses (like commission) meets that profit goal. Keep in mind that even if the resulting net comes below your goal, if all else with the offer looks good, you can renegotiate the price—or reduce the incentives, if you've offered any—to make up for the monetary gap.

Remember that it's typical for sellers to help with closing costs and many buyers expect it as a gesture, so don't be quick to cut that out of the deal. Instead consider

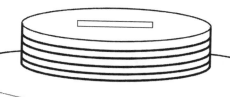

TIPS

Handling Multiple Offers

In a good market, you may face the mixed blessing of multiple offers. If this happens to you, don't be fooled into thinking that the best price is automatically the right choice. There are numerous factors that make for the best offer among many, factors like how the buyers' motivation, their financial qualifications, what extras and incentives they want, et cetera.

Discuss all the offers with your real estate agent to make sure you really do take the best of the bunch.

negotiating down any fixes that came up in the inspection that the buyers could do without or that they would be willing to handle themselves later on.

Step 3: The Inspector (Maybe).

If you said "yes" to the offer, the buyer—or the mortgage lender they're working with—might arrange for an inspection to be done on the home to confirm the property's condition.

Mortgage companies want to assure the property they're financing is worth the number that's listed on paper, and buyers may want the same reassurances when it comes to making as huge an investment as buying a house.

In light of all this, know that not every sale goes through a post-offer inspection. In some places this home inspection happens beforehand; in others places and in different circumstances (like with seller financed purchases) it may not be performed at all.

Each locale has its own rules, which is why having a real estate agent with knowledge and experience makes all the difference in smoothing out the sales process.

Step 4: More Yeses and Nos.

Depending on how previous negotiations and inspections went, you may have more things to consider before accepting the offer and moving forward with closing.

However, hopefully there won't be too much more. Negotiating can be the most aggravating part of selling a home since there's a lot of waiting, anxiety, and uncertainty about what the other party will decide and do—accept or counter?

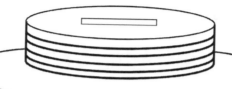

TIPS

Save Money by Getting a Pre-Inspection

The saying goes that sometimes you have to spend money to make money and that's generally the case when it comes to having a pre-inspection done on your home.

If you're selling your home as a fixer upper a pre-inspection doesn't pay off since that type of buyer is actively seeking a project.

However, if you're selling as a turn-key or close to, a pre-inspection can save you both time during the negotiations portion of a sale and money that you might otherwise spend on rushing unforesen fixes.

Try to keep things brief. Some buyers are turned off by too much back and forth and may, if things go on for too long, decide to back away from the purchase. The same goes for some sellers, because dealing with buyers who seem to love having the last word on negotiations can be tedious.

Don't frustrate buyers by taking too much time to make decisions, either. Be attentive, but don't rush forward and sell yourself short.

Again, this is where the expertise of your agent comes in: They'll have a sense about what the other party is expecting, and how much negotiating they'll be willing to take.

Step 5: Be Quick About It!

Generally, buyers want to get in their new house pronto, so don't dally on getting forms signed and paperwork in. Show them you're serious about selling and are respectful of their time[line].

As previously mentioned, some decisions must be made within predesignated time frames as outlined in the sales documents. Make note of these time frames and pay close attention, lest you lose the buyer's interest (or simply irritate them by defaulting upon the time sensitive terms of the contract) and have to start looking for another one.

One good way to keep yourself on track is to make a table of the predesignated time frames, write in the dates as they come, and post it somewhere obvious that you'll see it every day (e.g. your bathroom mirror or next to your daily calendar).

Often these timelines are not so much a specific date

and time, but rather a specific *number of days* following the previous action. For instance, when an offer comes in you may have anywhere from 24 hours to a few days to give an answer on it. If you respond before the final day, the clock for the buyer to respond in-kind begins when you give your answer, *not* on the would-be last day of the initial time period.

I encourage you to create a visible time table for yourself that you'll see every day if you think it'll help you stay organized and on track with deadlines and decisions. A chart like that also makes for a handy milestone marker, helping you to realize that things really are progressing, as sometimes the negotiating and paperwork processes can feel tedious, redundant, and never ending.

You can, of course, rely fully on your real estate agent to remind you about upcoming decision-making deadlines, but it'll be helpful if you're already looking ahead, prepared with a decision before they call with an urgent need for an answer.

##

Notes

In Closing.

By now you should be comfortable getting your property ready to sell and feel able to prepare your home in a way that earns you the most profit upon closing.

As mentioned in the Introduction, this book is designed so you can find what you need easily, with graphic icons strewn throughout to visually direct you to tips, reminders, and other relevant information you can use; a glossary to quickly look up definitions to common real estate concepts and terms; and an index of subjects so you can flip directly to the proper section of information. Also, if you purchased the print edition, its compact size fits easily in a glovebox, purse, or briefcase.

Use the Lists section following this chapter to quickly find tables and worksheets that were referenced in the book. The Appendix includes charts and templates that can help with the prep and sale of your property.

Also, if you happened to gloss over the scenarios included in the Story Boxes, I urge you to flip back and enjoy those narratives. They're actual circumstances and events that have happened to buyers and sellers I've known and worked with; knowing those stories may help you see how a concept I've described works—and could benefit you—in a real-life situation of your own.

Whether you read this book straight through or piecemeal, keep it close by to assure you sell your home for the most amount of money in the shortest amount of time.

Good luck, and happy selling!

##

Lists.

Tables

#: Name	Page
Table 1: Index of Special Markers	15
Table 2: Getting a Pre-Listing Home Inspection	50
Table 3: Staging Your Home for Sale	83
Table 4: Holding An Open House	108
Table 5: Is This Buyer *Serious* or *Not*? How to Tell.	141

Worksheets

#: Name	Page
Worksheet A: The Seller's Why, When, & How	35
Worksheet B: Walk-Through Checklist	59

Appendix.

THE ESSENTIAL GUIDE TO SELLING YOUR HOME's
30-60-90-DAY PRICE CHANGE SCHEDULE
template

Let's work together toward the sale of your home.

While the market will indicate the best sell price for your home, the first 30-day time period is the most critical when it comes to attracting the attention of buyers. This price change schedule enables us -- you, the seller, and your real estate agent(s) -- to market and sell your property at the highest price and as quickly as possible.

By agreeing to this schedule, you commit to working with us on pricing your property at Fair Market Value according to the suggested timeline.

Starting Price _____ Date _____

30-Day Adjustment _____ Date _____

60-Day Adjustment _____ Date _____

90-Day Adjustment _____ Date _____

_____ _____
Seller Signature   Date

_____ _____
Seller Signature   Date

_____ _____
Listing Agent Signature   Date

DISCLAIMER: Use of this worksheet does not guarantee the sale of your property within the proposed time period. This worksheet is only a tool to assist with the planning of your property's listing and should not be used or construed as a promise, guarantee, or warranty of the sale of or price received for the sale of any property.

THE ESSENTIAL GUIDE TO SELLING YOUR HOME's
D.I.Y. HOME INSPECTION
template

Let's work together toward the sale of your home.

While a home inspection report from a Certified Home Inspector may be required by a lender prior to sale, I always encourage sellers to inspect their homes themselves in order to (1) help them decide what they should and should not repair prior to listing or sale and (2) to provide useful information to potential buyers about the condition of the property.

This document is by no means a complete inspection report, but it can serve as a useful tool to track home improvement project progress or during purchase negotitations with buyers.

Bedrooms

MASTER	Good ✓	Needs Work ✗
Ceiling Fan		
Closet		
...*Rods*		
...*Shelving*		
Electrical		
...*Lighting (permanent)*		
...*Outlets*		
...*Switches*		
Flooring		
Walls		

DISCLAIMER: This worksheet is not an official document and does not guarantee the condition of the property located at the stated address on the designated date. This worksheet is only a tool to assist the home owner with the sharing of the designated property's condition as it appears to the home owner and should not be used or construed as a promise, guarantee, or warranty of the present or future condition, value, or use of any property.

THE ESSENTIAL GUIDE TO SELLING YOUR HOME's
D.I.Y. HOME INSPECTION
template continued

Bedrooms

Windows & Doors		
Other: _____		
Other: _____		

BEDROOM #2	Good ✓	Needs Work ✗
Ceiling Fan		
Closet		
...*Rods*		
...*Shelving*		
Electrical		
...*Lighting (permanent)*		
...*Outlets*		
...*Switches*		
Flooring		
Walls		
Windows & Doors		
Other: _____		

BEDROOM #3	Good ✓	Needs Work ✗
Ceiling Fan		
Closet		
...*Rods*		
...*Shelving*		

THE ESSENTIAL GUIDE TO SELLING YOUR HOME's
D.I.Y. HOME INSPECTION
template continued

Electrical		
...Lighting (permanent)		
...Outlets		
...Switches		
Flooring		
Walls		
Windows & Doors		
Other: _____		
Other: _____		

Kitchen, Baths, and Utility Rooms

Mark if the item shows problems.

PLUMBING & WATER	Kitchen	Bath 1	Bath 2	Utility
Hardware				
...Drain (sink)				
...Drain (tub)				
...Faucet (sink)				
...Faucet (tub)				
...Showerhead				
...Other: _____				
...Other: _____				
Pipes (under sink)				

THE ESSENTIAL GUIDE TO SELLING YOUR HOME's

D.I.Y. HOME INSPECTION

template continued

...*Active dripping*				
...*Corrosion/Rust*				
...*Water damage*				
...*Other:* _____				
Toilet				
...*Bowl*				
...*Tank*				
...*Other:* _____				
Other: _____				
Other: _____				

Electric

Mark if the item shows problems.

OUTLETS	Kitchen	Bath 1	Bath 2	Utility
Outlets				
...*Damaged or missing covers*				
...*Non-functional*				
...*Other:* _____				
Switches				
...*Damaged or missing covers*				
...*Non-functional*				
...*Other:* _____				
Other: _____				
Other: _____				

D.I.Y. HOME INSPECTION
template continued

Living Spaces

Mark if the item shows problems.

	Entry	Hall	Living	Kitchen
Baseboards				
Built-in Shelving				
Ceiling Fans				
Crown Moulding				
Fireplace				
...Firebox				
...Hearth				
...Mantle				
...Surround				
Flooring				
...Broken planks or tiles				
...Needs cleaning				
...Peeling/Scuffs/Tears (linoleum)				
...Other: _____				
Walls (paint, dents, etc.)				
Windows & Doors				
...Frames				
...Glass				
...Hinges, Latches, or Locks				
Other: _____				

THE ESSENTIAL GUIDE TO SELLING YOUR HOME's
D.I.Y. HOME INSPECTION
template continued

Other Areas

GARAGE	Good ✓	Needs Work ✗
Doors		
...*Exterior Access (from yard to garage)*		
...*Garage Door (main)*		
...*Interior Access (from house to garage)*		
Floor		
Lighting		
Outlets & Switches		
Permanent Fixtures (*e.g. shelves, workbenches, tool racks*)		
Walls		
Windows		
Other: _____		

STAIRS	Good ✓	Needs Work ✗
Flooring		
Railing		
...*Damaged or Loose*		
...*Not to Code*		
...*Other:* _____		
Walls (*paint, scuffs, holes, etc.*)		
Other: _____		

THE ESSENTIAL GUIDE TO SELLING YOUR HOME's
D.I.Y. HOME INSPECTION
template continued

BASEMENT	Good ✓	Needs Work ✗
Door *(exterior)*		
Door *(interior)*		
Electrical		
...Lighting		
...Outlets		
...Switches		
...Other: _____		
Floor		
Stairs		
Walls		
Windows		
Other: _____		
Other: _____		

THE ESSENTIAL GUIDE TO SELLING YOUR HOME's
D.I.Y. HOME INSPECTION
template continued

Part 2: Exterior

HARD *(Permanent)* FEATURES	Good ✓	Needs Work ✗
Chimneys		
Deck(s)		
Doors		
...Front (Main)		
...Back #1		
...Back #2		
...Other: _____		
Driveway		
Electrical		
...Light Fixture(s)		
...Outlets		
...Other: _____		
Fencing & Gates		
Faucets & Hoses		
Gutters		
Outbuildings & Sheds		
Patio(s) & Porches		
Retaining Walls		
Sidewalks & Permanent Walkways		
Siding		

THE ESSENTIAL GUIDE TO SELLING YOUR HOME's
D.I.Y. HOME INSPECTION
template continued

Windows		
Other: _____		
Other: _____		
Other: _____		

SOFT *(Nonpermanent)* FEATURES	Good ✓	Needs Work ✗
Drainage *(e.g. ditches, drains)*		
Flowerbeds & Gardens		
...Drainage		
...Mulching		
...Soil		
...Other: _____		
Furniture		
Hanging Pots & Planters		
Lawn		
Lighting *(e.g. solar path lights, string lighting, outdoor paper lanterns)*		
Paths & Walkways		
Shrubbery		
Trees: SEE NEXT TABLE	—	—
Other: _____		
Other: _____		

THE ESSENTIAL GUIDE TO SELLING YOUR HOME's
D.I.Y. HOME INSPECTION
template continued

TREE-SPECIFIC QUESTIONS	NO	YES	NOTES...
Any trees need soil, mulch, a trim?			
Any dead trees that need removing?			
Any sick or dying trees?			
Any trees too close to...			
...Main Home?			
...Neighboring Properties?			
...Outbuildings?			
...Sidewalks, Driveways, or Walkways?			
...Street, Streetlights, or Powerlines?			
Any trees <u>currently</u> causing foundation problems?			
Any trees <u>currently</u> causing roof or gutter problems?			
Any low hanging branches that need to be trimmed right away?			
Any branches or roots growing across your property line(s) into neighboring property?			

Tree-Related Notes: _____

_____

_____

_____

_____

_____

THE ESSENTIAL GUIDE TO SELLING YOUR HOME's
D.I.Y. HOME INSPECTION
template continued

Part 3: Appliances & Furnishings

Appliances

Environment Control	Stays	Good ✓	Needs Work ✗
A/C Unit(s) - Permanent	X		
A/C Unit(s) - Window/ Portable			
Air Purifier(s)			
Humidifier(s)			
Space Heater(s)			
Other: _____			
Other: _____			

Laundry Room	Stays	Good ✓	Needs Work ✗
Clothes Rack - Mobile			
Dryer			
Washer			
Other: _____			
Other: _____			

THE ESSENTIAL GUIDE TO SELLING YOUR HOME's
D.I.Y. HOME INSPECTION
template continued

Kitchen	Stays	Good ✓	Needs Work ✗
Dish Washer *(countertop or in-cabinet)*			
Microwave			
Oven/Stove			
Refrigerator			
Toaster Oven			
Utility/Microwave Cart			
Water Dispenser *(mobile)*			
Wine Rack/Cabinet			
Other:_____			
Other:_____			

Other	Stay	Good ✓	Needs Work ✗
Box Fan			
Fire Pit			
Hot Plate			
Mini- or Wine Refrigerator			
Patio Heater(s)			
Other:_____			

THE ESSENTIAL GUIDE TO SELLING YOUR HOME's
D.I.Y. HOME INSPECTION
template continued

Furnishings

	Stays	Good ✓	Needs Work ✗
Bedroom Sets			
...Bedroom 1			
...Bedroom 2			
...Master Bedroom			
...Other (e.g. basement bedroom)			
Bookcase(s)			
China Cabinet/Curio			
Coffee Table(s)			
Desk(s)			
Dining Table & Chairs			
File Cabinet(s)			
Gaming (*e.g. pool table, dartboard, pinball machine*)			
Recliner(s) & Sofa(s)			
Window Treatments			
Other: _____			
Other: _____			

. . .

This is the end of the template.

. . .

174

Glossary.

30-60-90-Day Price Change Schedule
A predetermined schedule depicting three 30-day price drop intervals for a listing designed to speed the sale of a specified property by maintaining buyer interest over the duration of that property's listing. Though advantageous to sellers, this system of pre-planned price drops is not common to all real estate agents or offices.

Accept (Acceptance)
The term used to indicate an agreement to the terms of an offer has been met (in other words, accepted). Upon acceptance of an offer, both buyer and seller are bound to complete the sale; if either party backs out after acceptance, monetary or legal consequences could ensue.

Appraisal
The estimated property value calculated by an appraiser.

Appraiser
A professional trained in seeking out and identifying all aspects of a property in order to determine that property's current market value.

Building Code
A set of rules determined by governing authorities that specify the standards for constructed objects.

Buyer Incentives
Premiums in the form of merchandise (e.g. appliances) or discounts offered to the prospective buyer before or during negotiations in the hope that this bonus will motivate the purchaser.

Closing Costs
Expenses above and beyond the price of the property in a

real estate transaction.

Closing Date

The scheduled day on which the sale of the property will be finalized and ownership will be transferred to the purchasing party.

Comparative Market Analysis (CMA)

A report compiled by a real estate agent that consists of various computations and analyses of data using comps and other property sales dynamics to help the agent and property owner(s) make best judgements when it comes to listing a home for sale.

Comps

The selling prices of comparable homes in the area.

Contingency

A condition that must be met before a sale can be finalized. Common contingencies include passing the home inspection, appraisal contingencies, or financing contingencies.

Cost of Doing Business

The cost of acquiring, producing, or maintaining a product for business purposes (cost is loosely defined as money, time, or energy).

Direct Mail Marketing

Marketing that uses a mail service to deliver a promotional printed piece – brochures, catalogs, postcards, newsletters and sales letters – to your target audience.

Down Payment

The out-of-pocket money paid toward a home before the

lender provides a loan to cover the rest of the purchase amount.

Earnest Money

The money provided by buyers along with an offer to purchase as a show of good faith. Earnest monies usually account for 1-2% of the home's purchase price. Upon the finalization of the sale, earnest money goes toward down payment. If the seller rejects the offer, the money is returned to the buyers. If the buyers back out, the seller keeps the money.

Encroachment

A type of encumbrance where one property intrudes onto another. For example, a detached garage is built over property lines; a fence or driveway crosses property lines or impedes required easements or right-of-ways around the property's perimeter. See also: *Encumbrance*.

Encumbrance

Any lien, claim, or liability attached to a property that may lessen its value or affect the transfer of said property's title.

Equity

The difference between a home's market value and the unpaid mortgage balance. In simple terms, the actual amount of the home actually owned by the owner. Equity generally increases over the life of the loan (as the owner pays more into the property), although can decrease if the housing market takes a negative turn, thus resulting in negative equity. See also: *Negative Equity*.

Fair Housing Act of 1968

A Federal (United States) law passed in 1968 that makes it illegal for sellers of property to refuse to sell or rent a dwelling to any person because of race, color, religion, sex, familial status, employment status, or national origin.

Fix
Differentiated from "renovating," fixing refers specifically to the repair of a broken feature. Example: Fixing a sagging beam or leaky pipe.

Fixer-upper
A property which require renovations or improvements in order to bring it to turn-key status.

Flipping
A type of real estate investment strategy in which an investor purchases property with the goal of reselling it for a profit.

For Sale by Owner (FSBO)
The process of selling real estate without the assistance of a licensed real estate agent.

Hashtag
Words or phrases preceded by a hash symbol (#) that are used in online and social media outlets to identify messages on a specific topic.

HVAC
Short for Heating, Ventilation, and Air Conditioning.

Inspection
An investigation conducted by a qualified home inspector that checks on the overall condition of a property

being sold.

Lead
A prospective buyer or seller who has been targeted through information sharing and/or collecting.

Lien
When a legal claim is held against a property in order to receive payment for debt. Lienholders can choose to sell the property in order to recover monies owed.

Listing
A home "listed" on the market for sale. Listings include basic information about the home for buyers to consider (e.g. square footage, age, price, number of bedrooms).

Market Value
The highest estimated price a buyer will pay and a seller will accept for a property an open and competitive market. In the simplest terms, the market value is the price at which both seller and buyer find agreeable and settle upon during a property's sale. Market values help establish trends in the real estate marketplace and can affect the values of nearby properties, whether or not those properties are intended for sale. See also: *Value*.

Multiple Listing Service (MLS)
A marketing database set up by a group of cooperating real estate brokers that lists properties for sale.

Negative Equity
When the value of a home is less than the remaining balance of the loan. Also known as being "underwater". Homeowners with negative equity are said to be "upside-down". See also: *Equity*.

Net Profit

The profit taken after expenses, losses, and other costs are considered.

Nose blind

A term used to describe the desensitization of a person's sense of smell to specific scents that they're constantly exposed to. Ex: An individual who keeps cats will eventually stop smelling (or stop noticing the smell of) their cats' litter boxes.

Open House

A scheduled event wherein a listed property is made available for viewing by prospective buyers without them having to make an appointment.

Owner Will Carry (OWC)

A financing option where the seller becomes the bank and negotiates a payment plan (including down payment options) with a prospective buyer.

Pre-Approval Letter

One step further than a pre-qualification letter, a pre-approval letter is an official notice from a lender that guarantees approval on a mortgage loan for a specified amount. To obtain this letter often involves an in-depth analysis of the buyer's income, credit, and assets, among other things.

Pre-Listing Inspection

A thorough inspection done by either the homeowner or a licensed home inspector that determines if any areas of the home need fixing or are not to code. A pre-listing inspection is usually followed by a written report that is made available to real estate agents and potential buyers as a reference.

Pre-Paid Utilities

Those utilities that the current owner can offer as a buyer incentive by pre-paying for services, usually done as a balance left on the utility account. See also: *Utilities*.

Pre-Qualification Letter

An official notice issued by a lender that outlines what a buyer can afford in terms of maximum loan amount and purchase price. This letter does not mean the buyer will be automatically approved for a loan, but is an indicator of the buyer's willingness and ability to purchase.

Predictable Factors

Factors that affect a selling season that can be reasonably predicted. Examples: weather, societal activity (holiday seasons), family status and related activities. See also: *Unpredictable Factors*.

REALTOR®

REALTOR® is a registered trademark of the National Association of Realtors (NAR). When a real estate agent associates themselves with this trademarked designation, it means they are a member of the NAR and must abide by the association's standards and Code of Ethics. Not every real estate agent is a REALTOR®.

Real Estate Agent

A person licensed to sell and/or rent out buildings and land for clients.

Renovate

Differentiated from "fixing," renovating refers to the improvement or updating of a home's feature that wasn't necessarily broken. Example: renovating (improving) kitchen countertops from laminate to marble.

Reverse Contingent Offer

A real estate strategy by which the seller makes an offer to the buyer instead of the buyer making an offer to the seller.

ROI (Return on Investment)

A measurement of a business's or investor's performance calculated by dividing net profit by net worth (or net investment). In real estate, it's a simple way to determine whether an investment will or has yielded a profit.

Selling Season

The season within your home's market and/or area that defines when during the calendar year your home has the greatest potential for being sold for the greatest price.

Social Media

Websites or electronic applications that allow users to communicate; create and share content; and network with other users.

Staging

The act of preparing of a private residence for sale through the arrangement of furnishings and décor with a goal of making a home appealing to the highest number of potential buyers.

Sweat Equity

A term used to describe any non-financial investment (usually in the form of manual labor, i.e. "sweat") put into a home to increase the home's market value.

Targeted Marketing
When marketing efforts are concentrated on buyers whose needs and desires most closely match your home's qualities and assets.

Title
A group of rights a property owner has over their property. These rights are generally transferred to the new owner(s) upon sale.

Title Insurance
An insurance policy that protects owners and lenders against property loss or damage due to problems with the property's title.

Turn-key
A subjective term which refers to a property that is 100% finished and ready for a buyer to move into. What qualifies as turn-key differs from person to person, but the term generally indicates a property that someone can simply bring their belongings into and immediately live in.

Unpredictable Factors
Factors that affect a selling season that cannot be reasonably predicted. Examples: changes in area demographics, mortgage interest rates, housing supply and demand. See also: *Predictable Factors*.

Utilities
Private or public services such as gas, electricity, cable, internet, telephone, water, garbage, and sewer that are provided as part of the development of the property. See

also: *Pre-paid Utilities*.

Value

The most probable price a property can bring in according to an appraisal report or other official valuation. See also: *Market Value*.

Walk-Through

An informal inspection performed by a homeowner that helps to determine what areas of the home require fixing or renovation.

Zoning

(1) Laws that define how real property can and cannot be used in certain areas. (2) How governments control the development of land and the ways in which that land can be used, usually to specify an area's activities (e.g. commercial, recreational, agricultural, residential, et cetera).

##

Index.

Term	Page(s)
HVAC	74
L	
leads	134
M	
market value	48, 118
MLS (Multiple Listing Service)	19, 88, 96, 120, 125
N	
net profit	148
nose blind	110
O	
open house	102, 104-114, 118, 134, 159
P	
pre-approval letter	132
pre-listing inspection	48, 52, 55, 57, 90
pre-paid utilities	125
pre-qualification letter	132
predictable factors	30, 31
R	
REALTOR®	5, 13, 82, 96, 100, 192

##

About the Author

Richard Cordaro

Richard "Rich" Cordaro has worked as a successful real estate agent since 2003, with a 30-year sales career spanning real estate and industry.

As a Listing Specialist and Realtor® of the Hershey (PA) and surrounding areas and founder of Find Hershey Homes, Rich takes great pride in helping home buyers and sellers achieve their real estate goals, and feeds his strong passion for bringing young people's professional and personal dreams to fruition by teaching real estate and business at the community college level.

A father of two and an avid sailor, Rich resides in Pennsylvania. He can be reached by email at

RCordaroBooks@gmail.com.

##